SUCCESSFUL   L OR

C000319818

WITHDRAWN FOR SALE 75p

Other How To Books on business and management

Arranging Insurance
Be a Freelance Sales Agent
Buy & Run a Shop
Buy & Run a Small Hotel
Communicate at Work
Conduct Staff Appraisals
Conducting Effective Interviews
Doing Business Abroad
Do Your Own Advertising
Do Your Own PR
Employ & Manage Staff
Investing in People
Investing in Stocks & Shares
Keep Business Accounts
Manage a Sales Team
Manage an Office
Manage Budgets & Cash Flows
Manage Computers at Work
Manage People at Work
Managing Meetings
Managing Yourself

Market Yourself
Master Book-Keeping
Master Public Speaking
Mastering Business English
Organising Effective Training
Prepare a Business Plan
Publish a Book
Publish a Newsletter
Raise Business Finance
Sell Your Business
Selling into Japan
Start a Business from Home
Start Your Own Business
Starting to Manage
Taking on Staff
Understand Finance at Work
Use the Internet
Winning Presentations
Write a Report
Write Business Letters
Write & Sell Computer Software
Your Own Business in Europe

Further titles in preparation

The How To series now contains more than 150 titles in the following categories:

Business Basics
Family Reference
Jobs & Careers
Living & Working Abroad
Student Handbooks
Successful Writing

Please send for a free copy of the latest catalogue for full details (see back cover for address).

BUSINESS BASICS

SUCCESSFUL MAIL ORDER MARKETING

How to build a really cost effective
operation from scratch

Ian Bruce

AS YOU CAN SEE, WE'VE HAD
QUITE A GOOD RESPONSE!

How To Books

Cartoons by Mike Flanagan

British Library Cataloguing in Publication Data
A catalogue record for this book is available from the British Library.

© Copyright 1996 by Ian Bruce.

First published in 1996 by How To Books Ltd, Plymbridge House,
Estover Road, Plymouth PL6 7PZ, United Kingdom.
Tel: (01752) 202301. Fax: (01752) 202331.

Note: The material contained in this book is set out in good faith for
general guidance and no liability can be accepted for loss or expense
incurred as a result of relying in particular circumstances on statements
made in the book. The laws and regulations are complex and liable to
change, and readers should check the current position with the relevant
authorities before making personal arrangements.

Produced for How To Books by Deer Park Productions.
Typeset by PDQ Typesetting, Stoke-on-Trent, Staffs.
Printed and bound by Cromwell Press, Broughton Gifford, Melksham,
Wiltshire.

Contents

List of Illustrations

Preface

We live in an age where self-sufficiency and financial independence are becoming increasingly important. Jobs are not nearly as secure as they were 20 years ago, and for this reason many people decide to take control of their own futures by turning to self-employment.

But even self-employment is no guarantee of success or stability. As large corporations begin to monopolise the traditional high-street markets, small and medium sized businesses are being put under immense pressure. Rent and rates for retail premises are rising, and at the same time profit margins are being cut to the bone. In the world of traditional marketing, only the strongest and wealthiest survive.

What the would-be self-employed person needs is a way of marketing products or services which can be started with a minimum of capital. A way in which he or she can compete with the 'big boys' on an equal footing right from the very beginning. A way which offers unlimited potential for expansion and prosperity, but a minimum of risk.

This book reveals such a way of doing business.

Mail order marketing is fast becoming one of the most popular and effective ways of selling goods and services to the general public. It is a unique form of business which can give freedom, flexibility and financial independence.

This ground-breaking manual will show you how to start your own mail order operation with a minimum of capital and build it into a highly profitable business within months. It contains scores of techniques and strategies which have, until now, been closely guarded secrets. It is a book which can give you the financial independence and security you need in today's world.

Read it and reap!

Ian Bruce

IS THIS YOU?

Wholesaler   Retailer

                    Ambitious

Manufacturer   Writer

                    Independent

Self-employed   Unemployed

                    Persuasive

Creative   Outgoing

                    Organised

Disciplined   Confident

                    Artistic

Sales person   Consultant

                Good communicator

Enthusiastic   Positive

                    Competitive

Practical   Redundant

                    Retired

Employed   Freelance

                    Homeworker

Craftsman   Inventive

                    Administrative

1
Setting Up In Business

DEFINING MAIL ORDER MARKETING

Mail order marketing is the term used to describe the selling of goods and services by mail. Prospective customers are reached through various forms of media advertising, such as newspapers and magazine adverts, or by a carefully written sales letter. Orders are then received and fulfilled via the postal services. It is an established marketing strategy which is fast becoming one of the most popular ways of moving products and services, and it has been said that eight out of ten adults have made at least one purchase by mail order during their lifetime.

Why is mail order so popular?

From the customers' point of view, mail order is popular because they can make a purchase without having to leave their home and travel to a traditional store. Instead, all they need to do is:

- complete a simple order form

- write out their cheque or credit card details

- post these items in the envelope provided.

Within a week or two their order will be delivered to their door by their postman. In short, mail order offers customers a method of ordering valuable products and services which is extremely **convenient**.

From your point of view, mail order marketing is a business which can easily be set up and run without the need for large amounts of starting capital or any previous business experience. It is a business which allows you to:

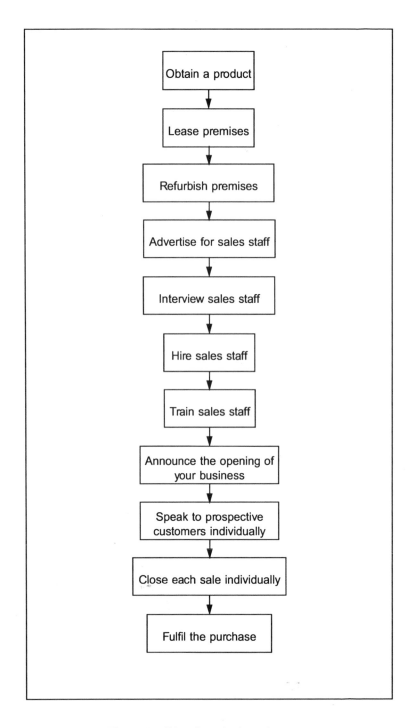

Fig. 1. Traditional marketing sales route.

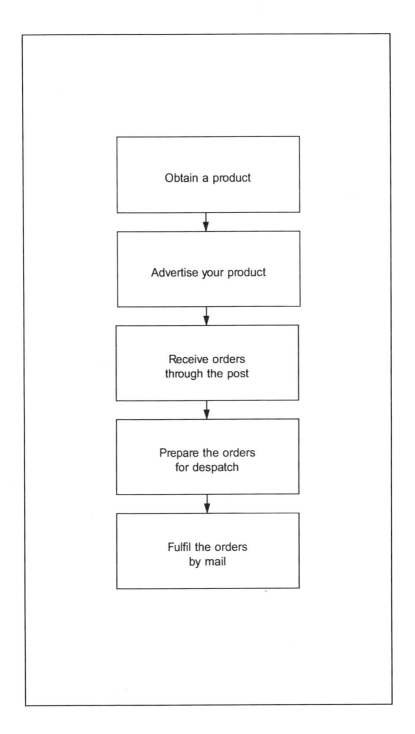

Fig. 2. Mail order marketing sales route.

- be your own boss

- work the hours you choose

- obtain financial independence.

It is a business which can be started on a small-scale, part-time basis from the comfort of your own home, but still has the potential to grow into something much, much bigger as your skills and experience develop.

Traditional marketing *vs* mail order marketing

When most people think about starting their own business, they think of opening a store and following the traditional sales route of physically placing products and services into the hands of their customers. Few ever consider running a mail order marketing business, even though this would involve a lot less capital and preparation.

To understand just how mail order marketing differs from the more traditional marketing method of selling through a high street store, we need to compare the sales routes used by these two forms of business (see Figures 1 and 2).

It is obvious to even the most untrained eye that mail order marketing is a far simpler and more cost-effective way of selling products and services than operating a traditional high-street business.

- Prospective customers are not reached by individual salespeople, but *en masse* via media advertising and/or direct mail.

- This reduces (and often eliminates) the need for a dedicated team of sales staff.

- Because customers are dealt with entirely by mail, the need for expensive retail premises is also eliminated.

These are just some of the reasons why mail order marketing is becoming the number one option for people who would like to set up their own business but do not have the capital or experience which is necessary to set up, operate and succeed with a traditional high-street store.

Why start a mail order business?

The main reason why it is advisable to begin a mail order business as opposed to a more traditional business is its **simplicity**. The essential ingredients for a successful mail order company are:

- a suitable product or service

- a place to stock products

- a place to work in

- a flair for (or willingness to learn about) marketing.

Since this book will teach you how to go about obtaining a suitable product or service and market it effectively by mail order, the only thing you need to set up and run your own business is a place to store products and work in. If you have a garage, converted loft or spare bedroom then this would be ideal, but if not, take a look at where there might be space for you to stock just a few products to get you going. You can tackle the pleasurable problem of expansion when it arrives.

Starting small

For those of you who think that starting your business from home may be a disadvantage, I urge you to think again. Many people have launched a mail order business on a small-scale, part-time basis with a minimum of capital, and watched it grow into a cash-rich organisation within months. In fact some very famous business people owe a lot, if not all, of their success to their involvement in mail order marketing.

Richard Branson is one such example. After launching a literary successful but largely unprofitable magazine called *Student* in his late teens, Richard decided that business was his passion, as opposed to journalism. With this in mind, Richard set up a small company under the name of Virgin Mail Order. He purchased bulk quantities of popular music and then made it available to the general public at discounted prices by advertising in the national media.

Success came swiftly, and as his newly formed enterprise grew from strength to strength, Richard began to think about opening a recording studio and releasing records on his own label called Virgin Records. The rest, as they say, is history.

What can I sell?

There are few limits to the variety of products and services which can be effectively marketed using mail order. Take a look through a magazine such as *Exchange & Mart* and you will find hundreds of mail order companies selling office supplies, marital aids, books, newsletters, tools, computers, life insurance and even garden gnomes, to name just a few. In a very real way, the products and services which can be offered by mail order marketing are limited only by the imagination of the person operating the business.

EXPLORING THE PROS AND CONS

All forms of business have both advantages and disadvantages. As far as mail order marketing is concerned, the advantages are almost always in the majority, which is good news for anyone who wants to start their own successful business with as little risk as possible.

Advantages

- A mail order business can be run from home, at least initially, so there are no expensive retail premises to lease or refurbish.

- You can begin with a minimum of capital. Your first media advertisements can cost just a few pounds, and your first sales letters can be created on a standard electronic typewriter or word processor.

- You do not have to have your own product or service in order to succeed. Many mail order companies buy their products very cheaply from one or two major suppliers and concentrate solely on marketing them for profit.

- Because you can start small, you won't have to store too many units of product to begin with – just enough to get your business off the ground.

- In mail order, you are on an equal footing with established companies right from the word go. Since customers will only know you by the image your marketing efforts portray, it is relatively easy to project the image of being much larger than you really are, and start making big profits within weeks.

- Because you reach potential customers using media advertisements and direct mail, you are not limited to selling your product or service within your own locality. Marketing your wares on a nation-wide basis is as simple as booking an advert in a national periodical or spending a few more pounds on national sales letters.

- If you are already in business for yourself, you can begin a mail order operation whilst continuing to use your existing marketing methods. This will allow you to experience greater profits without having to totally restructure your current organisation.

- A mail order marketing business will give you freedom from the nine-to-five 'rat race'. You will be your own boss, working when you want, where you want, for however long you want. You will have independence and be in total control of your life.

Disadvantages
- With total freedom and independence comes total responsibility. Your mail order business cannot succeed without your hard work and effort, and there is no possibility of you being able to 'pass the buck' of responsibility onto someone else.

- You will be sacrificing any regular pay check or salary which you currently receive. If your business succeeds then there is absolutely no limit to the financial prosperity which you can enjoy. But if your business fails then you may find yourself without any income whatsoever. To avoid this situation, many people begin their mail order business on a part-time basis, whilst continuing to enjoy the financial stability of their regular salaried job.

- In this business (as you would expect) marketing is everything. In order to succeed you will need to develop your talents. You will need to develop your creativity. You will need to learn the rules of effective communication which will provide you with a steady stream of orders and enquiries for your wares. Fortunately, this book contains everything you will need to know about effectively marketing products and services by mail order, so all you need to contribute is a little enthusiasm.

Mail order marketing has a phenomenal amount to offer the entrepreneurial spirit. Financial independence in your own business is yours for the taking. The way to take it is to follow the advice in this book and have a strong desire to succeed.

CREATING A PLACE OF WORK

Your place of work – as we have previously said – could be a spare bedroom, garage or converted loft. Some people have launched successful businesses by working at their dining room table too, so don't worry if you can't set aside a whole room initially.

Eventually you may need to move your business into an office building, but by that time your success will have provided the necessary funds, so once again, don't worry about it at the moment. For now, just make sure that you have the following facilities.

Storage space

As well as having enough space reserved to store your products, you should also set aside space for all the **paperwork** your business will generate, such as order forms, letters, *etc.* A standard filing cabinet is ideal for storing such paperwork and a suitable one can often be purchased very reasonably from an office clearance company or similar. Look out for such a unit in the classified or business section of your local newspaper. For the time being you can use a spare cupboard and simple box files available from any stationery stores.

Working space

Since your mail order business will involve a lot of paperwork, a **desk** should be high on your list of priorities. The style of desk is irrelevant, but try to make sure that it is sturdy and practical. Desks with drawers and cupboard space are ideal. Again, until you find a desk which suits you, use your dining room or kitchen table.

Communication facilities

Initially, the only essentials are:

- an electronic typewriter

- a telephone

- a telephone answering machine.

These will be your prime means of communicating not only with your suppliers and (occasionally) customers, but also with the advertising offices of the media which you will come to use. Your typewriter especially should be as good as you can reasonably afford so that the image you project to others is as professional as possible.

Optional extras

As your business grows you may want to upgrade your working equipment. Some items you should consider purchasing at a later date include:

• a word processor with good quality printer

• a fax machine

• a franking machine.

DESIGNING A PROFESSIONAL IMAGE

Image is everything in the world of mail order marketing. Your customers and competitors will judge you both by the way your stationery looks and by the way you speak on the telephone. It therefore makes sense that you should spend some time designing a professional image which will help you to succeed.

Business name

What you call your business depends largely on what you intend to sell by mail order. You can use your own name or create a totally separate company name, but either way you must ensure that it helps to describe your professional services.

• If you intend to offer a service of some kind, and you wish to build a reputation around your own name, it is wise to use your name as the basis of your business name. For example, if your name is John Smith and you wish to establish yourself as a consultant, a business name such as John Smith Consultancy Services would be ideal.

• If you wish to sell a product then it is better to omit your personal name and focus solely on the product. For example, Photo USA could be used for a company which specialises in selling photographs of the USA in the form of posters and postcards.

By the time you have finished reading this book, you should have a fairly good idea of what you would like to offer by mail order. If this isn't the case, or if you think that you may change your mind in the near future, select a business name which is broad enough to cover any such changes. Direct Trading is quite a vague name but still suggests that you are a mail order product-oriented company.

Stationery

Once you have decided upon a business name you can begin to think about obtaining your office stationery. This is where projecting a professional image is vital. If you send letters on onion-skin paper then no matter how neat your typing is, you will give the impression of being an inexperienced company which cannot even afford a standard weight of paper.

The easiest and most economical way of obtaining quality stationery is to purchase a 'business starter pack' which many printers offer. A typical pack comprising 200 professionally printed A4 letterheads, compliment slips and business cards can be purchased for between £50 and £100, and will be more than enough to successfully launch your business. Companies which offer such packs can be found in *Exchange & Mart* or your local *Yellow Pages*.

Telephone technique

As soon as you launch your business you will begin to use your telephone on a regular basis. More often than not, you will be speaking with suppliers and advertising offices rather than clients, but your telephone manner is vital nevertheless.

The rule of thumb when using the telephone is to act like a **professional**. Answer in your company name and be confident. On no account should you act as though you are taking a personal call. Remember, you are running a business in which the image you project is everything.

Recording an outgoing message

You should always pay close attention to the outgoing message which you leave on your answering machine.

- Try to make it sound as professional and courteous as possible.

- Avoid long pauses and hesitations.

- Be aware that background noise can often make your message sound amateurish.

If you have not yet purchased an answering machine then look for a model which has a pre-recorded outgoing message on it. These give a very good impression and can save hours of trial and error.

LAUNCHING YOUR BUSINESS

You have created a place of work and designed a professional image, so now all that remains is for you to launch your business and begin your journey towards mail order marketing success. The first step is to decide whether you will run your business as a limited company or as a sole trader.

Starting a limited company

Setting up a limited company can be quite complex and for this reason it is always advisable to consult a solicitor before taking the plunge. You will need to have your proposed company name checked to make sure that it isn't already being used by someone else, and then you will need to complete a few forms and return them to Companies House in Cardiff, along with a small administration fee.

As a limited company, you will need to:

- hire the services of an accountant to prepare and submit a set of accounts to both Companies House and the Inland Revenue each year

- carefully observe and abide by certain rules and regulations which govern the running of a limited company.

The main **advantage** of becoming a limited company is that you have limited liability as far as loss is concerned. In other words, if your business collapses all company assets may be seized and offset against any debts it has, but your personal assets will be left untouched unless you have used them as collateral on any business loans, *etc.*

Becoming a sole trader

Becoming a sole trader is by far the easiest way to set up a business, and because of this it is the route which is recommended to anyone embarking on mail order marketing for the first time.

To become a sole trader all you need to do is advise the relevant authorities of your new status and open a suitable business account with a bank (more on these topics below). You are then free to make a start on building your business in earnest.

As a sole trader you can:

- prepare you own accounts without using the services of an accountant

- change your trading status to that of a limited company once your business has become established

- minimise the amount of red tape you have to deal with.

Registering for tax and National Insurance contributions

Whichever form of trading status you choose, you must inform both the Inland Revenue and the Department of Social Security of your new circumstances. Simply write a letter to each (your local offices are listed in your telephone directory) and at the same time ask for any information which will be of use to you in the future.

Having received your notification, both offices will then amend their records and send you a few simple guides which explain how your tax and National Insurance contributions will be assessed and collected in the future.

Obtaining banking facilities

In order to keep your business income and expenditure separate from your personal finances, you will need to open a business account. All major high street banks offer such accounts, but each has its own level of charges, and these can vary wildly.

Before choosing who to bank with, you should shop around as much as possible and find an account which suits both your needs and your pocket. Also make sure that you read the small print relating to any account which you intend to open. The last thing your new business will need to cope with is banking charges which you weren't expecting.

General insurance

It is important to take a second look at your current **home contents insurance** policy to check if business equipment is covered or not. In most cases it won't be, and you will have to take out a separate insurance to protect business assets such as your typewriter or word-processor, *etc.*

If you are confident that you could – if necessary – replace your current equipment quickly (and without too much of a financial burden) you may choose to survive without a separate insurance policy during the early days. If, on the other hand, losing your typewriter (for example) would threaten your business survival, taking out adequate insurance to cover such an event is vital.

If you are in any doubt about your need for specialist business insurance, discuss your situation with your financial adviser or insurance broker.

Now that we have covered the basics, let's present the steps to launching your own business in the form of an easy-to-follow flowchart (see Figure 3).

CHECKLIST

Could you succeed in mail order marketing?

- Are you ambitious?   Yes/No

- Would you like to achieve financial independence?   Yes/No

- Would you like to be your own boss?   Yes/No

- Are you willing to develop your creativity?   Yes/No

- Are you willing to develop your communication skills?   Yes/No

- Can you be self-disciplined?   Yes/No

- Can you organise yourself?   Yes/No

If you answered yes to four or more of the above questions then there is no reason why you cannot set up and run your own highly successful mail order marketing business. Follow the advice contained in this book and you have it in your power to give yourself and your family a wonderful future.

CASE STUDIES

Throughout the course of this book we will be following the progress of three people as they learn to succeed with their own mail order marketing businesses. Each one has embarked on their own mail order business for a different reason and in different ways. Together the case studies will show you how the information in this book can be applied to a variety of situations.

Richard Stanford takes the plunge

Richard is in his 30s and has spent the last ten years writing

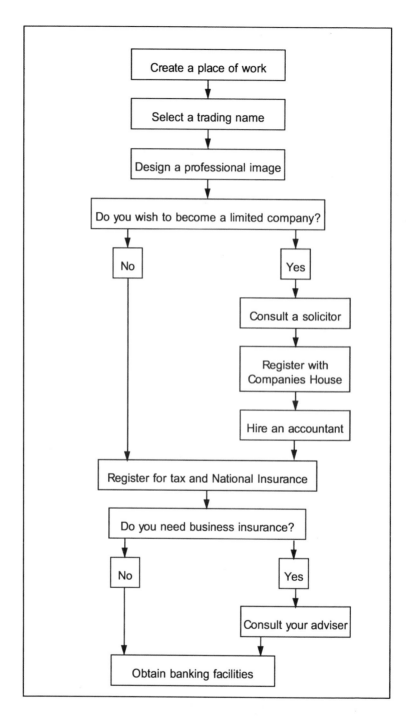

Fig. 3. Launching your business (flowchart).

computer software for a medium-sized company. He enjoys his work but feels that he is not being sufficiently rewarded for his efforts. He has considered starting his own business writing and selling computer software but the large amount of capital involved in recruiting sales staff and opening a specialist store has always been a stumbling block. At the same time, if he allowed someone else to publish and market his work he would be no better off than he is now.

Richard comes across the concept of mail order marketing and the potential of setting up and running such a business appeals to him. He decides to start a mail order company called 'Software By Mail' as a sole trader, but continues working for his employer so that he can retain a sense of financial security.

Pauline Sherring dips her toes in the water
Pauline is a housewife who has been thinking about returning to work for some time. She is a qualified chef and would like to get involved in catering once again. However, Pauline has two small children to look after and cannot find a suitable position which offers the flexible hours she needs.

When Pauline hears about mail order marketing she realises that she could set up a small company selling catering equipment and work the hours that are most suitable to her. Initially she intends to work on a part-time basis and store her products in the garage, but would eventually like to see her company reach its full potential. She starts out as a sole trader using the name of 'Direct Catering Equipment'.

Alex Foley goes limited
Alex has been running his own small business as a music tutor for over 14 years, but for the last few years he has become increasingly concerned at the reducing number of students who visit him. After making some enquiries Alex concludes that many people now prefer to learn to play their instruments at their own pace by studying books and watching instructional videos in the comfort of their own homes.

Knowing that his business will die unless he adapts to the current market, Alex visits his solicitor and forms his own limited company 'Treble Clef Ltd'. His intention is to continue giving personal tuition to those who request it, but at the same time to sell instructional videos, books and compact discs to students by mail order. This will allow him to profit from the developing home study trend without having to sacrifice his existing business activities.

DISCUSSION POINTS

1. Why do you want to start your own business?

2. Why would a mail order marketing business suit you?

3. What qualities do you have which you think would help you to succeed in your own mail order business?

2
Creating Your Product

In all forms of marketing, be it mail order or more conventional high-street retailing, the product or service which you sell is of vital importance. No matter how effective your marketing campaign is, long term success can only be built on a product which adds value for your customers. If you strive to give your customers **quality** and **excellence** then your business will flourish, but if you set out to use mail order marketing as a way to off-load poor products or services, you are setting yourself up for failure.

Creating a product which has the greatest chance of being successful is quite a simple matter. In fact there are just four main steps which you need to take. These are:

- analyse the **existing market**

- generate **ideas**

- identify a market **niche**

- obtain an **original product** which fits this niche.

ANALYSING THE MARKET

Analysing the mail order market will enable you to see what type of products and services are already being marketed successfully by other companies. It will highlight products which are particularly successful, and others which are beginning to wane in popularity. In brief, it will allow you to identify the market area which you are most likely to succeed in.

To analyse the market yourself, all you need to do is take an active interest in what is happening in the world of mail order. Do this by:

- Studying the newspapers, magazines and journals which frequently carry the advertisements of other mail order companies.

27

Books

Cassettes   Videos

Compact discs

Garden supplies   DIY tools

Computer accessories

Stationery   Foodstuffs

Gifts

Pictures   Fine china

Rare coins and banknotes

Clothing   Cosmetics

Marital aids

Insurance products   Printing services

Toys

Car accessories   Health supplements

Pet supplies

Office supplies   Sports equipment

Fine wines

Fig. 4. The established market.

- Making a note of what is being offered by each. Note the price of the product, the target audience, and the benefits which the product is said to give.

It won't be very long before you begin to see that some products are advertised more often than others. These products will normally belong to one of three market categories:

- the established market
- the 'fad' market
- the new market.

The established market category

This category usually has the lion's share of the mail order world. The products and services advertised in this category have been tried and tested over many years and are seen by many as being the most reliable for a new mail order company to depend upon.

The list of products and services shown in Figure 4 is not by any means exhaustive. It merely represents the tip of the iceberg as far as the established mail order market category is concerned. Literally thousands of other products and services also come under this category, and you will discover these as you analyse the market for yourself.

If you are new to mail order marketing then you would be wise to start by selecting a product or service which has proven success in this sector of the market – and preferably one which lends itself to repeat purchases. These are consumable items which satisfied customers will order again and again, such as office stationery, and are an excellent way to establish a regular inflow of business.

As your business grows you may then wish to expand into one of the other two market categories.

The 'fad' market category

The 'fad' category has long been part of the mail order world, but with the nature of the 'fad' being what it is, the products offered in this category vary considerably. Over the past ten years the fad market has offered whoopee cushions, whistling key rings, buoyant soap and even plastic cigarettes (for people trying to give up smoking). Today's fad market offers lottery gizmos, gambling systems, new-age crystals, lucky amulets, executive toys and a whole host of other imponderables.

There is no doubt that a mail order company can achieve great success in the fad market category, but doing so takes considerable skill. The trader would need to be able to spot a potential 'fad' before it becomes common knowledge and jump aboard the 'gravy train' in time to collect his rewards.

All too often beginners in the mail order world jump aboard obvious 'gravy trains' just as the fad has reached its peak of popularity. The result is that they get their fingers burned and end up with a garage full of sponge mallets (or something equally useful) that can't even be given away.

This being the case, you are strongly advised to **avoid** getting involved in the fad market until you have gained plenty of experience with more established products and services.

The new market category

New markets are those which are created by public demand. Before the advent of the home computer there was no demand for mouse mats or floppy disk drive cleaners. However, within just a few years of the launch of personal computers, these items began to sell like hot cakes. The public themselves created this new market because they demanded accessories for their new purchases.

Identifying a new market whilst it is still new is not easy by any means. It generally takes a lot of study and more than a little creative thinking – but it can be done.

If you wish to 'discover' a new market whilst it is still young, you need to be aware of the products and services which are due to be launched. Read articles in the trade press. Look at the American mainstream mail order market (which is often just a year or two ahead of our own) and see what is developing there. Such intense market study sometimes pays great dividends, but again, it is best left alone until you have some practical experience in the established market category.

GENERATING IDEAS

By the time you have analysed the current mail order market, you should have a fairly good idea of what is being sold to the majority of customers, and by whom. All you need to do now is come up with an idea for a similar product of your own which will enable you to exploit these existing markets.

Do what you love – a key to success

One of the keys to success in mail order marketing is 'do what you love'. This is because the easiest way to come up with a quality product or service is to concentrate on a market which reflects your own personal interests.

If you have a **hobby** or **pastime** which you are passionate about, focus your attention on this. Begin to think about products as a consumer rather than a trader, and ask yourself questions such as:

- What product or service would make your hobby more enjoyable?

- What might make it more practical, economical of efficient?

- How would having such a product or service benefit you?

- Does the product or service already exist?

- If not, is there any reason why it shouldn't succeed?

- If a product already exists, could it be improved in any way?

- Could the product be enhanced to make it more appealing?

Your answers to such questions will often help you to generate an idea for a product which has potential. If not, ask other people who share your interests to comment on the above questions. If you find that the same sort of answers come up regularly, this indicates that a market exists for a specific type of product or service.

IDENTIFYING A NICHE

Once you have analysed the existing market opportunities and defined a product or service which you think would satisfy a public demand, you should study a little further in order to identify a niche within the market.

This niche is the sector of the market which is most likely to buy your product or service when it is launched. Get it right and your business will grow rapidly into a cash-rich organisation. Get it wrong and success will be much harder to achieve.

Create a customer stereotype

The most effective way of identifying a niche is to create a customer stereotype. To do this, you should once again imagine that you are a typical customer. From this perspective, take a piece of paper and write down the answers to the following questions:

- How old are you?

- Are you male or female?

- What specialist magazines are you most likely to read on a regular basis?

- What is your average level of income?

- What attracts you to a product or service?

- Why?

Continue to question yourself in this manner so that you begin to 'flesh out' the psychological make-up of a typical customer. When you have finished, this stereotype will enable you to know what the majority of your potential customers want, how much they are prepared to pay for it and, in brief, what makes them tick.

Armed with this information, you can then obtain a product which meets those needs and desires as closely as possible. This will ensure that the product you choose is one which already has a niche market (made up of people who closely resemble your stereotypical customer) which is waiting for it, and success will come swiftly.

OBTAINING YOUR PRODUCT

Once you have identified the type of product which is most likely to do well in a specific market niche, all you need to do is obtain it, name it and sell it. There are three basic ways of obtaining your product. You can:

1. Develop a **new product** from scratch. This will involve designing, testing, patenting and manufacturing an idea, and will demand large quantities of time, money and effort. It is the most complicated route to success in the mail order world, and therefore best suited to people with substantial mail order experience.

2. Take a **basic idea** which has already been marketed successfully via mail order and give it a 'twist'. Add a little something which will make the product more practical, unusual or desirable. Again, this route to obtaining a suitable product will take time and effort but is not as complicated as designing a new product from scratch.

3. Obtain a **ready-made product** from a reputable wholesale supplier or a manufacturer. For total newcomers to the world of mail order marketing who want to sell a product which is already being sold successfully by other companies, or for people who have trouble generating original ideas, this option is usually the most effective. The product will already have been 'tested' by your competition, and your success is almost guaranteed if you can market it effectively. Sources of existing products can be found in trade magazines such as *Exchange & Mart*, *The Dealer*, *Wholesaler* and *The Trader*.

NAMING YOUR PRODUCT

The name which you give to your product is immensely important. Try to make it as **specific** as possible. If your product is a telephone which glows when ringing, then say so. Do not be tempted to call it an 'Inert Gas Communications Module'. Prospective customers won't have any idea what you're talking about, and if you confuse the customer you dramatically reduce your chances of making a sale.

Even though you shouldn't revert to 'hype' tactics when naming your product, it is important that the name should convey a sense of dynamism wherever possible. Thus, if we stick with the above example, 'The Amazing Neon Telephone' would work well, particularly if aimed towards the teenage or novelty sector of the established market.

PRICING YOUR PRODUCT

The price of your product is equally vital to the success or failure of your business. If you charge too much then you may not receive as many orders as you need to make a profit. If, on the other hand, you charge too little, you may well find it difficult to make a profit even with a moderate response.

The art of pricing your product is to tread a fine line between too little and too much. This can be quite difficult to master, but if in doubt it is always recommended that you err towards charging too much. This might sound a little unconventional, but read on and you'll see that it makes perfect sense.

Face value and perceived value
One problem which many beginners face when pricing their products is that they do not understand the difference between

face value and perceived value. Without this fundamental under-
standing it is impossible to make money in mail order marketing.

If you sell (for the sake of example) books that cost £10 to
produce, and you price your product according to face value, you
would market them for £10 each. After your overheads have been
taken into account, you would make a loss. If you sell each book for
£15 in order to cover these overheads, you would simply break even.
But if you can make that £10 book worth £50 to the reader, you
enter the realms of profitability and mail order success. This is the
magic of selling products according to perceived value.

The question you need to ask when pricing your product is not
'How much did it cost me to acquire?' but 'How much value will it
give to my customers?' If your product in some way saves £200 a
year on fuel bills, then it would be reasonable to sell it for anywhere
in the region of £50–£200, even if you acquired it for just £10 or so.

Adding value

A standard rule of thumb is to try and ensure that you sell your
product for a *minimum* of at least three times the cost you paid for
it, and preferably more. If you don't think that you can make your
product worth that much to your customer then go back to the
drawing board – but not until you have read the rest of this book.
The fact is that skilful marketing can add value to almost anything,
so don't give up hope just yet.

If you think that charging considerably more than the face value
of a product is a low tactic, make a point of finding out how much
your everyday purchases actually cost to manufacture. Find out how
much it costs to make a compact disc, a computer game or portable
television. Then compare these 'face values' with the prices they are
sold at to the general public. You will soon come to realise that no
one sells products at their face values. Everyone has to have a wide
profit margin in order to run a successful business of any type, and
mail order is no exception.

Assessing customer demand

Another factor which you need to consider when pricing products is
the likely level of **customer demand**. If customer demand will be high
according to your market research, then you can afford to charge
more. If customer demand is likely to be low then you will have to
charge less in order to attract more interest.

Finally, you need to bear in mind the **availability** of your product.
If you are offering something which a customer can obtain only

from you, then you can set any price you wish, as long as there is a genuine demand for it. If, on the other hand, customers can get a similar version of your product elsewhere then your price obviously needs to be more competitive.

CHECKLIST

- Have you analysed the current mail order market as a whole?

- Have you decided which market category you would like to concentrate on?

- Have you generated an idea for a new product or service?

- Have you created a customer stereotype?

- Have you identified a niche within your chosen market?

- Have you decided how to obtain your product?

- Have you thought of a name for your product?

- Have you priced your product?

CASE STUDIES

Richard identifies his market

Because of his decade of experience in the computer software business, Richard doesn't have too much trouble analysing the current market. He knows what kind of products his competitors are concentrating on selling and is pleased that customer demand is high for new, innovative software.

One thing that does come to light during Richard's market research is the fact that no one offers an accountancy package which allows people to use the modern PC's speech recognition capabilities. He has written such a program for his own use, and decides that developing it would give him a great product to launch his new business with.

After several weeks, Richard completes the commercial software product. He obtains quotes for a professional package to be created from his master discs, and places a small trial order.

Within just a few months of first analysing the market, Richard now has a product to sell. 'Stanford's Speech Accounts' is the name of the product which he hopes will attract an avalanche of orders. After considering the competition and the perceived value of the product he has created, he prices the package at a competitive £199, even though it only costs him £27 to obtain.

Pauline opts for a pointed product

Knowing that she wants to start out on a small, part-time basis, Pauline begins looking at catering markets in order to identify a niche for a small product which can be stored easily.

She discovers that Swiss knives are in great demand, and that established mail order catering companies are selling sets of these at huge profits. After studying the trade press and wholesale journals, she locates a company which import such knives direct for just £15 per set, which is a fraction of their retail worth. Better still, the knives are guaranteed for ten years' use.

Pauline decides to purchase a modest quantity of stock to get her started and 'The Sherring Swiss Blade Set' is born, with a retail price of £79.99.

Alex hits the right note

After some thought, Alex decides that people want to learn music and not pay extra for flashy packaging. He identifies a niche for economy materials which aren't readily available in high-street stores.

'Treble Clef Tutorials' are packages containing a text book and either an audio cassette tape or compact disc, but without any expensive dressing. He prices these at just £29.99 (they cost him £6 each to obtain) and he hopes for a large number of orders to make this effective.

DISCUSSION POINTS

1. What product do you intend to sell, and why?

2. Why does the current market need such a product?

3. What name have you given your product, and what were your reasons for choosing this name?

4. How much are you asking for your product? Why do you feel that this price is appropriate?

3
Producing a Marketing Plan

A marketing plan is an essential tool in the mail order world. In its most common form, it is a simple written document which states:

- what product you intend to sell

- which sector of the market you intend to concentrate on

- what competition you will face

- what you will spend on marketing

- how much profit you hope to make

- what form of advertising you will use to reach potential customers

- what makes your product so special.

The more detailed and specific your marketing plan, the greater your chance of eventual success.

A marketing plan can be likened to a blueprint for success – or failure – depending on its quality. If you spend just a little time and effort in creating a solid plan, your business is more likely to succeed. On the other hand, if you are sloppy in creating a marketing plan, you cannot expect your business to be anything other than that.

LOCATING YOUR CUSTOMERS

In the last chapter you created your 'stereotypical customer'. Amongst other things you should have defined his age, income, habits, and desires, along with the publications which he is most likely to read on a regular basis.

At this point you need to make sure that your stereotypical customer is as well-defined as possible. In particular, you need to know:

- where he looks when he wants to purchase something

- what magazines he is likely to read on a regular basis

- what radio station he is most likely to listen to (if any)

- what would encourage him to make a mail order purchase

- what would discourage him from making a mail order purchase.

Knowing your customer

By the time you have fleshed out your character as fully as possible, you should feel as though you know him personally. In many cases you will, for your stereotypical customer may well be based on your own habits – particularly if you intend to sell a product or service which is related to your own interests.

To give you an example of what a stereotypical customer looks like on paper, let us imagine that you want to sell a directory of Internet sites to computer enthusiasts. In creating an appropriate stereotypical customer you discover that he is usually:

Your stereotypical customer
- male

- aged between 17 and 40

- intelligent and logical

- a subscriber to one or more computer magazines

- happy to read direct mail when it is related to computing

- eager to expand his knowledge of the Internet.

This information will help you to decide which marketing strategy to adopt (more of this later) and why. It will also give you confidence to go ahead in one particular marketing direction, and prevent you from advertising in publications which your potential customers are unlikely to read on a regular basis.

Knowing and locating your customers is a vital part of your marketing plan. Spend some time getting it right and you will stand head and shoulders above most mail order operators who operate solely on a 'wing and a prayer' basis.

LEARNING FROM YOUR COMPETITORS

The next part of your marketing plan should identify your competitors. These are the people who are selling similar products to you in the same niche market. Perhaps a company is already selling a successful Internet book? If so, examine this company carefully and find out:

• how much they charge

• where they advertise

• what type of advertising they do

• how much they spend on marketing

• how long they have been in business

• how many units they sell each year.

In order to obtain some of this information, you may need to make a few telephone calls, but the effort will be well worth it.

You might also speak to a few of your competitor's customers. Find out why they buy from this company. What are the perceived advantages (price, service, quality of product, for example) and disadvantages (*eg* slow delivery) of doing business with them?

Spotting trends

It is important to understand that no company can satisfy all of the people all of the time. It therefore stands to reason that some customers will be happier with the company than others. This does not really matter. Your job is to try and become a 'trend-spotter'. Look for repeated phrases that begin to shed some light on your competitors as a whole. If you discover that most customers love the product of your competitors but would appreciate a faster delivery, make a note of this – it could be your key to gaining an edge over them at a later date.

When you have studied your competitors as thoroughly as possible, note the main features of your study. Write down what makes them popular and what makes them less popular. Your goal will be twofold:

- to be at least as good as your competitors' good points

- to gain an advantage over them by exploiting their bad points.

DEVELOPING PROFIT AND COST PROJECTIONS

Now we get to the financial side of things and begin to prepare a simple projection of profits and costs. In the early days a new mail order company will have to complete this section based on educated guesswork, or even omit it altogether until the business is established.

If you wish to take the educated guesswork path, start with the figures which you already know:

- How much does your product cost per unit?

- How much does it cost to pack and mail one unit to a customer in the UK?

- How much profit does this leave after mailing?

Then begin to work with some more detailed figures. How many units need to be sold to make a £100 advertisement profitable? If you find out that one of your competitors makes a profit of £100 for every £100 he spends on advertising, how might your product compare?

Calculations like these can be misleading in the beginning. After all, you do not yet have the reputation which your competitors enjoy. Neither do you know exactly how many orders you can expect to get from one advertisement.

The aim of this section of the marketing plan is not to *dictate* but to *indicate* how much you stand to make if you can get a reasonable response to your advertising efforts. Once your business has been up and running for a month or two and you have some hard data to work from, this section of your marketing plan can be revised in order to make it more realistic and, therefore, more reliable.

FINDING YOUR UNIQUE SELLING PROPOSITION

Your 'Unique Selling Proposition' (USP) is the main quality or feature which makes your product different from those of your competitors. It is the answer which you would give to anyone who asks 'What's so special about this, then?' It is also the feature which you will concentrate on selling during the actual marketing of your product.

If you are the only mail order company which is willing to offer 48 hours guaranteed delivery then this is a USP. Others include:

- **price** – if your product is cheaper than those of your competitors

- **quality** – if your product is better than those of your competitors

- **service** – if you can serve your customers better than your competitors.

Fashions come and go but one thing remains certain: companies which know and convey their USP will always be more successful than those that don't.

Defining your own USP

To discover and define your own USP, spend some time answering these questions:

- Why should a customer buy from you and not from ABC Ltd?

- What makes your company so special?

- What does your product offer that ABC's doesn't?

If it happens that, after answering the above questions, you can't identify any particular USP then you should make it a priority to find one. Add a little twist to your product. Enhance the service you will give to customers. Do *anything* to ensure that your product has a Unique Selling Proposition.

To return to the example we used earlier in this chapter, maybe your Internet directory contains more listings than those of your competitors. Maybe you enclose a free computer disk drive cleaner with every order. Maybe you guarantee delivery in seven days or less. Maybe your customers can order over the Internet direct. If one of these facts is unique to your company, it is a USP, and will greatly increase your chance of success.

SELECTING A MARKETING STRATEGY

Finally, we come to the actual strategy which you will use to reach potential customers. There are three main marketing strategies in the world of mail order marketing, and these are:

- direct mail

- one step media advertising

- two step media advertising.

Direct mail

Direct mail is where you send a sales letter to potential customers without them having requested such information. The letter introduces your company and the products you sell. It describes your USP and tells the recipient why he or she should consider ordering from you.

A customer orders by filling in an order coupon included with the mailing piece and returning it with their payment. Normally you will receive at least a handful of orders within days of your customers reading your letter.

Direct mail is most effective in selling products which deserve a lot of text. If it is going to take three pages of text to explain just why your product is so good, and do it justice, a direct mail piece will be cheaper than taking out huge chunks of expensive advertising space in the national media.

If your stereotypical customer is willing to read unsolicited mail which is relevant to him then direct mail may well be a suitable strategy to adopt.

One step media advertising

This method involves placing a display advertisement in the media (usually a newspaper or magazine) which describes the product and asks for the order at the same time. Readers read the advert and then order off-the-page.

One step advertising does not allow you to spend as much space describing your product as a direct mail letter does, but it has a similar advantage of generating immediate response. Within days of your one step advertisement appearing – if your advertisement is effective – you should begin to receive orders.

If your stereotypical customer is often willing to order a product that appeals to him without first having to read through brochures or lengthy descriptions, one step advertising can be incredibly effective.

Two step media advertising

Using this strategy, a small display or classified advertisement is placed in a newspaper or magazine. This advertisement gives a brief summary of your product and invites the reader to ask for more information. When they do so you send them a sales letter (as with direct mail) which gives more detail and asks for the order.

Two step advertising is a little more time-consuming than the other methods we have discussed, but is generally very cost-effective. Because readers have to *ask* for the information about your product or service, you will usually only be sending direct mail to people who are genuinely interested in making a purchase. This helps to cut costs and increase the overall profitability of a marketing campaign.

Two step advertising is an ideal form of marketing for newcomers to the world of mail order. Initial expenditure is relatively low (due to the small cost of classified adverts) and this allows you to test various concepts without a high level of risk.

If your stereotypical customer likes to read information only when he has requested it, because he tends to be rather selective or busy, then two step advertising may best suit your marketing needs.

Which strategy suits you?

The marketing strategy you choose to adopt should be based on your capital and experience, and the preferences of your stereotypical customer. If you are already running a successful company you may wish to dive straight into mass direct mail or large one step display advertisements. If you are new to mail order, or are more cautious by nature, you will probably be drawn towards the cheaper and less risky two step advertising strategy until you have developed more confidence and capital.

Whatever strategy you choose to adopt, you can always test the water before you dive in at the deep end. You will learn how to do this later in the book. You should also note that you can change your strategy as and when the need arises. Remember, your marketing plan is meant to be a guideline – it is not a vow of eternal commitment to one business route over another.

Once your marketing plan is drawn up, it is time to set the wheels of your business in motion.

CHECKLIST

• Have you now fully defined your stereotypical customer?

- Have you investigated your competitors?

- Have you developed some initial profit and cost projections?

- Have you identified your Unique Selling Proposition?

- Have you selected a marketing strategy to start with?

CASE STUDIES

Richard goes direct

Richard is in the fortunate position of knowing the USP of his product right from the beginning. He already knows that there aren't any companies offering accounts software with a speech recognition capability, so all he really needs is to flesh out is his stereotypical customer.

Richard feels that the people who can benefit most from his software are professional accountants. After a little research he discovers that many of the major accounting firms have their own software suppliers which are tied to the chain of companies as a whole. It would therefore be rather pointless trying to sell his package to these firms. Instead, Richard decides that independent firms of accountants are most likely to be interested in Stanford's Speech Accounts.

As far as marketing is concerned, Richard realises that accountants are very busy people and have little time to give newspapers and magazines more than a passing glance, so he decides to contact his prospective customers by direct mail. This will allow the executives to read about his product in their own time and at their own pace. It will also give Richard the space he needs to accurately describe what he considers to be a revolutionary product.

Pauline does a two step

Finding a USP in her knives wasn't easy. After all, one set of Swiss knives is much like another. But then, her knives are guaranteed for ten years, and they are also competitively priced. After much thought, Pauline decides that 'Quality with Economy' is her USP.

Because she wants to start her business in a small way, Pauline decides that she will initially use two step advertising to launch her products. Her stereotypical customer (a semi-professional or professional chef with a budget to keep in mind) reads specialist catering magazines, and so she decides that this type of media would be most effective in reaching potential clients.

The only part of the marketing plan which she is having any difficulty with is the profit and cost projections. At this point she has no idea how well her knives will sell, and she cannot compare herself with the large companies who use one step advertising because they are obviously operating on a different level at this time.

She decides to calculate how many sets of knives she needs to sell to make her initial advertising profitable. In doing this she learns that if she sells just three sets of knives, she will make a small profit. This does not seem to be a great deal to hope for, and the strategy will with luck do somewhat better, but at least she now has some figures in mind to guide her.

Alex does it in one
To reach the number of potential customers which he needs to make his relatively low prices effective, Alex knows straight away that fairly large one step media adverts are the way for him to go. Having years of experience in the music business, he feels he has a good knowledge of his market and knows what music students want.

His main problem is knowing where to advertise. Should he concentrate on advertising in the music press, or should he go for a national newspaper and try to reach the millions of people who would like to be musicians if they had the opportunity?

Alex decides on the latter course. His main objective is to reach people who want to develop their latent musical talents, so restricting his offer to the people who are already subscribing to the music press would not be appropriate. One step general media adverts are the way to go.

DISCUSSION POINTS

1. Why is it important to have as complete a picture of your stereotypical customer as possible?

2. Which marketing strategy are you particularly attracted to, and why?

3. What are the main benefits of having a strong USP?

4
Using Direct Mail

Direct mail, as you learned in the last chapter, allows prospective clients to study your sales message at their own pace and in their own time. But before you stand a chance of making a sale, you must first overcome a major obstacle: the waste paper bin.

The fact is that if all mail order marketing companies targeted their clients properly, people would only ever receive mail which they find interesting or useful. Unfortunately, many companies (through ignorance or a desire to waste huge amounts of money) choose to 'blanket mail' a wide variety of people who find their sales letters to be irrelevant, inappropriate and subsequently annoying. Needless to say, the habit of many people today is to discard 'junk mail' as soon as – or even before – they open it.

Getting recipients of your letters to actually open the envelope is a fairly easy task, and we will look at techniques for doing this towards the end of this chapter. Far more difficult is making your sales message sound interesting and informative enough for them to continue reading it.

WRITING AN EFFECTIVE SALES LETTER

Let's step inside the mind of your stereotypical customer for a moment. He retrieves your mail package from his mail box, opens the envelope and . . . what next?

- If he begins reading what he believes to be 'just another sales letter' then your marketing material will be discarded faster than an old banana skin.

- If something he reads catches his interest immediately then he will probably read it or make time to do so later.

Studies have shown that what a potential customer reads within the **first five seconds** can make or break your whole marketing campaign. It therefore stands to reason that if you can make the beginning of your letter as irresistible as possible, you stand a far greater chance of getting an order at the end of the day.

Creating the headline
You should begin your letter with a headline. Forget what you learned at school about conventional letter formats and open with a strong, bold headline at the top of the page.

The headline can say whatever you want, but it is usually most effective if it does one of the following things:

Asks a question
For example,

WOULD YOU LIKE TO WIN THE POOLS?

would be a good headline if you wanted to sell a book about Treble Chance football pools winners and their techniques.

Creates intrigue
For example,

READ THIS IF YOU WANT TO STAY
ONE STEP AHEAD OF THE JONES!

might be used to sell the latest gardening gadget.

Makes a statement
For example,

SMOKING IS GOOD FOR YOU...

might be an eye-catching opening for a company which sells stop-smoking self-hypnosis tapes. The dramatic opening statement would probably continue along the lines of '... only if you are a major shareholder in a tobacco company'.

The most important point to remember is that the headline **must** make the reader want to continue reading the letter – even if it is just to find out what you're talking about. On no account should your headline indicate that this is a sales letter. A headline such as 'PLEASE BUY OUR LATEST GIZMO' would be effective only in

breaking the land speed record for your letter reaching the nearest
refuse site.

Drafting the introduction

If the headline succeeds in its purpose of grabbing the attention of
the reader, he will obviously begin to read the introduction to your
letter. This should be as fascinating as your product will allow so as
to develop even more interest and get your reader well and truly
hooked. In this section you should continue avoiding the sales
message and concentrate on developing the theme suggested in your
headline.

One interesting fact which you may want to keep in mind is that
readers can always be hooked if you play on one of three basic
emotions: greed, lust and fear. I know that this sounds rather
pathetic, but when you think of the most effective advertisements,
you will find that they all play on one of these three emotions in
some way.

Greed

The desire for more of what potential customers already have. More
money, more fun, more joy, more happiness, more success, a bigger
house, a faster car, *etc.* Commonly advertised products using this
emotion are cars, newspapers (via their competitions) and lotteries.

Lust

The desire for something which potential customers do not have,
but which they would like to have. Fame, fortune, romantic
encounters with supermodels and so on are good examples.
Commonly advertised products using this emotion are chocolate
bars, fragrances, clothes, hair products, jewellery and ice cream.

Fear

The desire of potential customers to avoid death, sickness, wrinkles,
poverty, homelessness and disability, or at least to prepare for such
occurrences. Commonly advertised products using this emotion are
insurance products, health care products, skin creams and pension
plans.

The most successful products are usually the ones which play on
two or three of the above emotions simultaneously. For example,
consider cars which are said to increase your sexual attractiveness
(exploiting lust), go faster than any other (exploiting greed) and
come complete with airbags (exploiting fear).

The introductory segment of your letter is the place to announce the emotion(s) you wish to play on. For example, if you still intend to sell an Internet site directory, you could probably play on the emotions of lust and greed quite effectively. Lust because your directory contains sites which no one else knows about, and greed because your directory contains far more sites than any of its competing titles.

Of course, it is important to remember that the whole of your sales letter must be legal and honest. Lying for the sake of giving your product more emotional appeal (drink this cola and get rich quick!) will not only sound unbelievable, but will also earn you a mighty slap on the wrist from the Advertising Standards Association for purposeful misrepresentation (we will discuss more of this in Chapter 9)!

So make your introduction as breath-taking and thought provoking as possible, but don't go overboard and start lying. Tell the truth, make a point of playing with the readers' buying emotions and the sales will follow automatically.

Using the right words

The words you use throughout the sales letter will affect the readers' emotions just as much as the message itself. For this reason it is important not only to think about *what* you write, but also about the way you write it.

Again, studies have shown that most readers like to 'obtain' products rather than 'buy' them. This subtle difference is a great one. The word *buy* tends to make the reader think of spending his hard earned money, but *obtain* makes him think of acquiring something. Hence one word stresses the negative part of the transaction (spending money) and the other stresses the positive aspect (obtaining something).

Professional copy-writers call words which stress the negative aspects 'cold words', and words which stress positive aspects 'hot words'. Figures 5 and 6 show two charts which reveal the most common hot and cold words. Avoid the cold words as much as possible and use the hot words instead. Your sales letter will be all the more effective.

Of course, these charts should only be taken as guidelines. In the mail order marketing world, rules are often broken and sometimes a deviation from the expected norm can increase sales considerably (for a wonderful example of this, watch the film *Crazy People* starring Dudley Moore and Daryl Hannah). Initially, however, it is

Practical

Free   Guaranteed

Proven

Unique   Genuine

Exclusive

Original   Reliable

Breath-taking

Attractive   Remarkable

Improved

Elegant   Desirable

New

Save   Valuable

Approved

Authentic   Secret

Invest

Dynamic   Sensuous

Impressive

Quality   Tasteful

Compact

Designer   Precious

Fig. 5. 'Hot' advertising words.

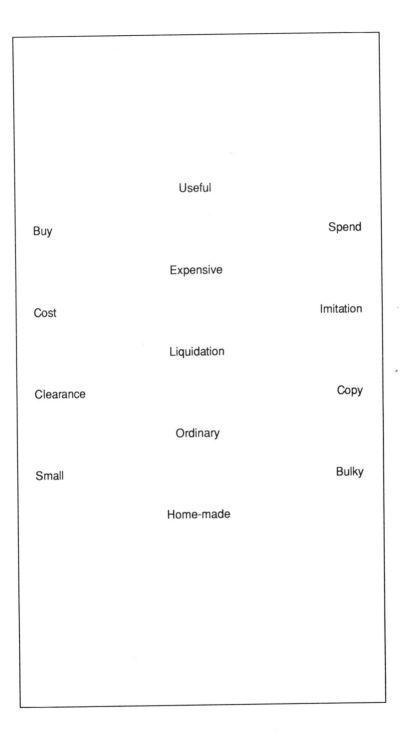

Fig. 6. 'Cold' advertising words.

advisable to follow the rules as closely as you can – especially if this is your first venture into the business world.

Writing the body copy

Once you have gained the interest of the reader by writing a powerful headline and introduction, you should then go on to write the body copy. This is where you may introduce your product and explain just why it would benefit the reader.

The benefits which you give should be as emotive, exciting and personal as possible, so that the reader can immediately identify your product as being something they want. Don't say 'This book explains how to save money and build a nest egg'. That's boring. Instead say 'This book reveals one of the greatest wealth-accumulation secrets used by the rich and famous!'. Don't say 'This computerised calorie counter will help you lose weight'. Instead say 'This amazing scientific breakthrough will help give you the body of your dreams!'.

Selling the sizzle

This is what is known as selling the sizzle instead of the sausage. No one buys sausages because they want half a kilo of dead animal in their refrigerator! Rather, they buy sausages because they like the aromas and sound of sizzling sausages, and the pleasure of eating them. They are therefore more concerned with buying the emotional appeal of eating sausages rather than the raw material itself.

The same is true of almost all products. Although people want their purchases to be useful, what makes them purchase initially is the emotion – or the sizzle – which accompanies that product.

If you do your job properly, your body copy will convince the reader that your product is just what he wants, needs or both. It will convince him not only of your product's usefulness, but also of its desirability and the emotional high he will experience when he owns it. All that's left to do now is close the sale and get the reader to send you his order.

Crafting the conclusion

This is where the conclusion comes in. Your conclusion should summarise the points you have made in the introduction and body copy, but make it brief. The last thing a reader wants to do is read your sales letter all over again!

Summarise the emotions you played on during the letter, and then sum up the benefits which your product gives. Announce that your

'[Insert your own hot word here]' product is now available and can be obtained by sending just £30 (or whatever), then print a neat order form for the customer to complete and return with their payment.

This is the standard structure for a sales letter, and when written well, orders will flood in. Having said that, nothing is ever perfect, so in a later chapter we will discuss more secrets which will help you increase the response rate your letters yield. For now, let us view the basic structure of a sales letter in the form of a flowchart (see Figure 7).

OBTAINING A MAILING LIST

Once you have written a sales letter to the very best of your ability, you will need to acquire a list of prospective customers. Mailing lists are sold by many professional **list brokers**, but some brokers are better than others. Before purchasing a list from a broker, make sure that he can meet the following criteria:

- he must have a good reputation and an established business

- he must be willing to provide references from satisfied clients

- he must keep his lists up to date

- he must be registered with the Data Protection Registrar.

The list

The list itself is the most important item to consider. Obviously the list should be made up of people who closely resemble the stereotypical customer you created earlier. It's no good buying a list that is cheap if it is made up of people who would never be interested in your products or services. Doing so would be a classic example of false economy.

Initially you would be unwise to purchase a complete mailing list of 50,000 or more names. Instead you should ask for a test list to make sure that it is viable as far as your product is concerned. A test list of around 5,000 potential customers will enable you to test the list as well as your sales package without too much of a financial risk.

PACKAGING YOUR OFFER

All that's left to do before you can test your product is to package

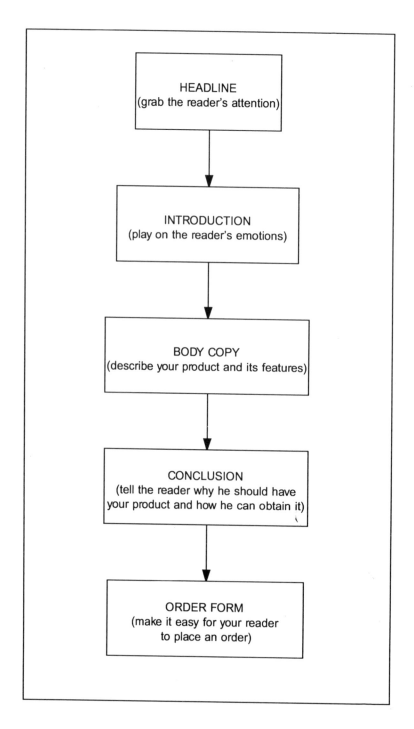

Fig. 7. Sales letter flowchart.

your offer attractively. Packaging your offer is just as important as packaging the products themselves, and must serve two main purposes:

- to inspire confidence in the professionalism of your business
- to protect the contents from damage.

Designing and printing

Get your sales letter printed professionally on good quality paper. If the printer is willing to help you typeset the letter for a small fee then this is a good service to have done at the same time. A professionally typeset and printed letter on 100gsm paper will make a good impression with its recipients and put you head and shoulders above the amateurs who insist on sending out poorly photocopied and poorly designed sales letters.

Choosing the right envelope

The envelope you use to send your letter in must also exude quality. It should be big enough to carry your sales letter comfortably, and strong enough to withstand the sometimes heavy-handed postal services. Thin brown envelopes, or ones which can only accommodate a sales letter which has been folded several times, are to be avoided at all costs.

Some mail order companies get their printers to print a line or two of text on the envelope (this is known as 'envelope copy') to encourage the recipient to open it. A line such as 'Private documents enclosed...' will intrigue most people and very few will want to risk discarding it without at least checking to see what the mysterious envelope contains.

Envelope copy is a very good tool to use as your business grows, but initially equally good results can be had simply by having the words 'private and confidential' printed on the envelope face. Some large stationery companies offer pre-printed envelopes of this type, and this can be an economical way to make sure that your sales letter gets opened.

TESTING YOUR OFFER

When you have your professional sales package ready to send, it is time to test it. If you have done your homework and followed the advice contained in this book, your test mailing should make a profit, or at the very least, break even.

Having said that, don't expect to know the *true* results of your test mailing immediately. Whilst most interested people will respond fairly quickly to your offer, there are always people who like to hang onto sales letters for a few weeks – and in some cases a few months – before finally having the 'courage' to send their order. Thus if a mailing list makes profit within two weeks of first sending it, you are likely to be on to a good thing, and a full mailing would be the next logical step.

If your test mailing hasn't made a profit within a month then you have either got to improve your sales package or obtain a more effective list, or both. Look at your letter first and try to improve it. If necessary, call on the services of a professional copywriter to help you.

Once you are satisfied that your letter is up to scratch, make sure that your list contains the right sort of people. As I said earlier, a poor list will make even the most effective sales package fail, so do a double and triple check to ensure that it is going to people who closely resemble your stereotypical customer.

Reaping rewards

Direct mail can be one of the most enjoyable and lucrative ways to advertise your products and services. The satisfaction of having written a dynamic sales letter and then to see your hard work reap rewards in the form of a flood of orders (and cheques) is unlike any other you are likely to experience in the business world.

Even if you intend to use media one step or two step advertising (which we will discuss in the next chapter) it is always necessary to learn to write effective sales letters, so do not neglect it. Without this skill you will have a hard time achieving success. With it, your success will be inevitable.

CHECKLIST

- Have you given your sales letter a good, attention-grabbing headline?

- Have you written an introduction which appeals to the reader's emotions?

- Have you used hot words wherever possible?

- Have you described the benefits of your product?

- Have you located a mailing list broker who is reputable and reliable?

- Does he have lists that match your stereotypical client?

- Have you packaged your sales letter in a professional manner?

CASE STUDIES

Richard makes it easy

The best thing about 'Stanford's Speech Accounts' is that it's so easy to use. Instead of clicking the computer's mouse buttons to move from document to document, an accountant can simply speak the commands directly into a desktop microphone. Knowing that time is money, and that his product makes it easy to save time, Richard writes a headline for his letter which reads

HOW TO TALK AND SAVE MONEY!

The letter continues by introducing the concept of time being money, and saved time being saved money. The introduction itself focuses on the fact that if an accountant can save just five minutes each day, he will save almost three eight-hour working days over the course of a year. This time could then be freed to attend to more clients, and hence the free time is converted into more money.

The emotion which Richard has concentrated on is greed, or the desire for more time and more money. As soon as he has made the recipient feel greedy (in the introduction) he goes straight into the body copy which introduces 'Stanford's Speech Accounts' as the perfect way to save time and make more money.

Pauline sharpens her skills

At first, Pauline can't see how anyone could feel emotional about kitchen knives, but after some thought she realises that not everyone uses the high quality Swiss blades that she is offering. She recognises that she can use lust to make her clients *want* the knives because these are the sort of tools which the most professional and highly respected chefs rely on regularly.

She conveys to her readers that they can now own top-quality professional kitchen knives at well below their true value. She uses the words 'valuable', 'guaranteed' and 'safe' throughout the body copy of her letter, and points out that cutting yourself with a knife is actually more common if cheaper, blunter knives are used. Thus she manages to work the emotion of fear into her letter too.

Although Pauline has no intention of using direct mail to sell her knives, she knows that she will still need to prepare a sales package to send to the people who respond to her two step advertising strategy, and so she writes with this in mind.

Alex sells potential

For years, Alex has watched nervous amateurs become confident musicians. He has seen how they value the positive comments of their friends, and how they enjoy being in the limelight.

Alex plays on this basic lust for musical success and admiration in his sales letter, which he will later use as the basis of his media advertisements. He encourages the readers to imagine the way people will react to them when they play a guitar solo in public for the very first time. He gets them to imagine the applause and the positive comments, and tries his best to make them feel as though they are already successful, accomplished musicians.

Then, in his body copy, Alex tells the reader that his products can make this dream a reality. Top quality music tutorials at amazing prices. How can the reader not give himself the chance to realise his latent musical potential?

DISCUSSION POINTS

1. Consider the emotions which professional advertisers use on a daily basis. Watch television commercials and ask yourself which emotions they are trying to appeal to.

2. Which commercials do you find most effective? Why do you think this is?

3. Can you think of other ways of giving your product more emotional magnetism? How?

5
Advertising Your Product

When using either one step or two step advertising to tell prospective customers about your products, the key issue of using emotion as a selling tool is just as applicable as it is to direct mail.

Using the one step advertising strategy, you place a display advertisement of one sort or another and aim to get an instant order. To achieve this, you need to be able to make the reader feel emotionally compelled to order right away. And because space is costly (a full page advert in a national newspaper would be well out of the reach of the average newcomer to mail order) you need to be concise as well.

Two step advertising is slightly different. You usually place a small advert which asks for only one thing: an enquiry. At this stage you are not seeking to sell your product. The only thing you should be selling is the idea of getting more information, but this still requires you to appeal to the emotions of your readers.

PLACING CLASSIFIED ADVERTISEMENTS

Newcomers to mail order often use two step advertising to test the water of their business. Advertising expense is kept to a minimum because your advert will be short – usually in the classified section of a magazine or journal. Direct mail expenses will also be low because you only send a sales letter to people who actually want to read it.

Placing classified advertisements, or small display advertisements in cheaper publications, is an art in itself. Just how do you get a reader to want to send you a self-addressed envelope in order to get more information?

Again, the answer is to play on one of the three basic buying emotions: greed, lust or fear. The headline should be eye-catching because it is likely to be surrounded by other similar ads. And it should also be compelling.

FREE MONEY

is a good, eye catching headline, and would perhaps be used by someone who is selling rare bank notes. The following copy could read something like 'A rare banknote will be sent to you if you send an sae to:' and the name and address follows.

This example classified advert is an excellent template. It attracts attention, plays on the emotions of greed (more money) and lust (free money) and compels a response. Another bonus is that the only people who respond to your advert are those likely to be interested in rare banknotes. Thus you can assume that around 90 per cent of the responses you receive will be coming from your stereotypical customers.

Time well spent

Just because a classified advertisement is small doesn't mean that you should spend less time preparing it. Invest at least an hour or two in ensuring that your classified ad is as powerful as possible. Then make sure that your advert contains the following elements:

- a powerful, attractive headline

- a play on greed, lust or fear

- an invitation to receive FREE details with no strings attached.

Because of the small cost of placing classified adverts, it is possible to refine your text by trial and error so that you create an ad which pulls in the maximum possible number of enquiries. Once you have such an advert, it can be placed in several publications simultaneously so that the number of enquiries you receive increases accordingly.

With two step advertising, the sales letter you send to enquirers is only slightly different from the one you created in the last chapter. You would obviously open with a powerful headline because the reader may well have lost the emotional feeling you stirred up in your initial classified ad. You would also refer to the ad in your opening paragraph, saying something like 'Thank you for responding to my recent classified announcement...' and then continue to hook your reader as before.

CREATING DISPLAY ADVERTISEMENTS

Display advertising is somewhat different. Using this strategy, the core of your sales message must be conveyed in a much smaller space than if you were using direct mail. This takes quite a lot of skill, but can be done very effectively with a little practice. The key is to keep waffle to a minimum and get to the point straight away.

Adapting your sales letter

To create an effective display advert, it is usually best to use the sales letter you created in the last chapter as a basic guideline. Follow this simple five-step plan to convert a full-blown sales letter into a more concise but equally powerful display advertisement.

1. Revise your **headline** so that it will stand out from the page and attract as many readers as possible.

2. Rewrite your **introduction** so that it gets straight to the emotional issue without undue hesitation.

3. Introduce your product in the **body copy** and emphasise its features and benefits. Using bullet points to do this will help to shorten sentences (thus saving space) and create a visually attractive advert.

4. Create a powerful **conclusion** which makes the reader want to order NOW. Keep in mind that if they do not decide to order as soon as they read the advert, they are unlikely to order at all.

5. Provide a **clip-coupon** at the foot of the advert so that the reader can act on his impulse immediately and contact you by return.

This format for display advertisements has been tried and tested over many years. Look at the mail order sections of the tabloid newspapers each weekend and you will see various examples of this format in action.

Incorporating illustrations

One good advantage of display over classified advertising is that display adverts allow you to incorporate graphical illustrations into your message if this would help to sell your product.

Obviously, not all products can be illustrated effectively. A booklet about bodybuilding is not likely to be visually impressive, but it is nevertheless valuable to certain members of the public. In cases such as this, you would be better off doing without an illustration and use the space to describe your booklet in more detail.

If your product is one which *is* visually attractive, however, an illustration can work wonders. Use one which captures the imagination and strengthens the emotions which you are playing with in the text of your advert. A picture of a designer suit on its own is rarely exciting to look at, no matter how well made. But a picture of the same suit being modelled by a young executive surrounded by two or three elegant and obviously impressed females will help the reader to associate your product with sexual attractiveness and success.

Sourcing illustrations
When providing illustrations, you can either use your own (if you have any) or obtain a suitable picture from a media library. These libraries are used to providing pictures for advertising purposes, and so will usually be able to help you find the image you are looking for – in return for a suitable fee, of course.

Placing illustrations
Actually placing the illustration in your advertisement needs a lot of thought. You cannot simply slap a picture anywhere on the page and expect it to be a success.

American psychologists who study the way the human brain works have theorised that if a reader has to look to the upper right hand side of a page to see a picture, that picture will make more of an impression on them. This has something to do with the way human beings process and store optical information. How reliable this theory is cannot be determined, but placing your illustration in the top right hand corner of your advert is quite convenient (only the headline and introductory paragraph need shifting to the left) and many mail order professionals claim that the strategy helps to increase significantly the number of orders which they receive.

Typesetting your display advert
In order to get professional results from your display advert, it must look professional. Always remember that your advertising materials are your ambassadors. If a multi-national company places poor quality advertising, it will be perceived as a poor-quality company irrespective of its actual standing. Similarly, if a young man who operates a mail order business from his bedroom places adverts which exude a professional image, customers will perceive his company as being professional, well-established and probably much larger than it really is.

For this reason you should have your advertisement typeset professionally. You can either deal with a professional typesetter and pay a fee for his services, or you can ask the advertising department of the media you wish to use to typeset the advert for you. Many will do this free of charge, simply because they know that the more successful they can help you become, the more money you are likely to spend on future advertising. Some, however, make a small charge for this service.

No one ever said that creating a professional, effective display advertisement would be easy. But if you spend an adequate amount of time and effort in creating one to the best of your ability, the rewards will be plentiful. Again, to help you visualise the process of creating a display advertisement, Figure 8 is a flowchart which illustrates the steps that need to be taken.

USING OTHER MEDIA

Although mail order marketing advertisements are more visible in printed media such as newspapers and magazines, other media can be used just as effectively. Here is a brief summary of the other main media which can be used to sell products or services by mail order. Whilst these types of media are not usually suitable for beginners, they may well prove to be profitable when your business is more established.

Television
Television adverts are effective in that you can reach millions of potential customers simultaneously. Some companies have great success in this medium, but you have to be big to be able to afford the incredible costs involved.

Another minus is that TV is only really suitable for products which are aimed at the masses. Using TV to reach a narrow niche of any market is very difficult, and some would argue that it is in fact impossible. Definitely not one for newcomers, but worth bearing in mind for when your success reaches dizzy heights.

Radio
Radio is not as expensive as TV as far as advertising cost is concerned, but it is still incredibly difficult to target a niche market using this medium unless you are willing to sponsor a particular programme on a commercial radio station. Thus our intrepid Internet directory merchant might sponsor 'computer news weekly' or something equally specialised.

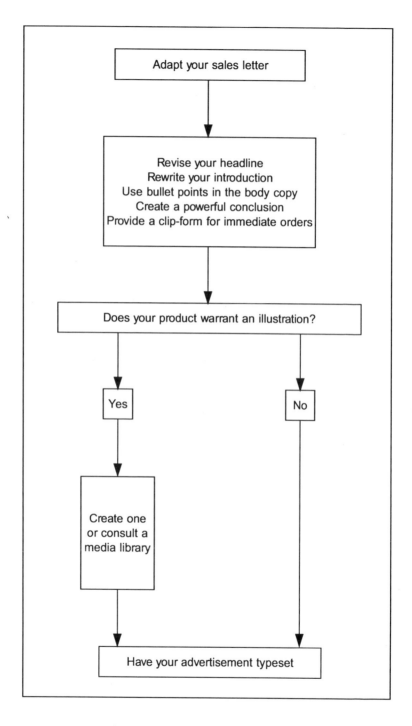

Fig. 8. Display advertisement flowchart.

Billboards

Large mail order catalogue companies use billboards to increase customer awareness of their name and products, but beyond that there is little use for billboards in mail order. After all, who wants to stand in the middle of the high street reading about the latest gardening gadget and making a note of the address to order from?

The Internet

The Internet is a world-wide network of computers which is becoming immensely popular. At least 20 million people use the Internet on a regular basis, and targeting niche markets in this medium is very simple and incredibly effective. If a product can be sold effectively via conventional media-based mail order then you can be sure that it can be sold effectively via the Internet and you should investigate this in greater detail.

The only downside is that most Internet mail order operators need to be able to accept credit card orders, so unless you already have this facility it is best to establish your business using conventional print media before entering this exciting market.

OBTAINING THE BEST DEAL

No matter where you advertise, you should always try to ensure that you get the best deal possible. For new companies in particular, positive cash flow is vital, and you will not want to pay over the odds for any particular advert.

The rule of thumb is always to ask for a discount – even if you already have one. Make the point that if your advert is successful, you may want to become a regular advertiser. Sometimes this tactic can save you a few precious per cent on the advert cost. At other times your request will be turned down flat, but you will have lost nothing for asking.

Shop around whenever possible, but remember that you usually get what you pay for. A very cheap advert is probably going to bring you very cheap results, but if you think that your advert will do well, give it a try. Most mail order businessmen seem to agree that a middle-of-the-road publication with middle-of-the-road prices will always be more effective than placing a cheap advert in a cheap publication.

CHECKLIST

- Have you created all of the necessary advertising materials for your chosen strategy?

● Have you selected the media outlet which is most suitable to your needs?

● Are you ready to get the ball rolling and start making money?

CASE STUDIES

Richard mails 5,000

Having acquired a test mailing list of independent accountancy firms and had his sales letter professionally typeset and printed, Richard puts together 5,000 packages and mails them. He mails them on Thursday by first class so that the letters will arrive on Friday morning. Hopefully, the recipients will be interested enough in his offer to want to read it over more fully over the weekend.

Richard knows that he has done everything by the book, and he is confident that his product will appeal to his target audience. All he can do now is wait and see if his confidence is justified.

Pauline goes classified

It took Pauline a while before she was totally satisfied with her sales letter, but after a few careful revisions she is now happy that it will be effective. She created several classified advertisements before finally settling for one which is short, punchy and attractive. The advert makes no mention of cost or even product detail, but will hopefully ensure that anyone who responds is interested in kitchen equipment.

She places the advert in a popular catering magazine and crosses her fingers, hoping that her efforts will prove to be fruitful.

Alex gets himself a bargain

It wasn't easy creating a display advert which said everything that he wanted it to say, but Alex managed it in the end. The final advert mixed solid feature/benefit text with emotional prose. To illustrate the advert, Alex contacted a media library and obtained a photograph of a guitarist receiving a standing ovation in a theatre setting. Hopefully, this image would make the readers feel ambitious and even more emotional about the product.

After making several telephone calls to advertising departments, Alex was offered a generous discount on a half page advert. Normally Alex wouldn't have been able to afford such a large advert, but the previous advertiser had cancelled his booking and the newspaper was eager to fill the space as quickly as possible.

The newspaper will print his advertisement this Saturday, and Alex is optimistic that his new mail order business will get off to a good start.

DISCUSSION POINTS

1. What are your feelings towards placing your first advert? Are you nervous or excited?

2. If you are nervous, why is this?

3. How could you improve upon your advertising materials? Would rewriting any of your materials give you more confidence in launching your business?

HOW TO DO YOUR OWN ADVERTISING
The secrets of successful sales promotion

Michael Bennie

'Entrepreneurs and small businesses are flooding the market with new products and services; the only way to beat the competition is successful selling – and that means advertising'. But what can you afford? This book is for anyone who needs – or wants – to advertise effectively, but does not want to pay agency rates. Michael Bennie is Director of Studies at the Copywriting School. 'An absolute must for everyone running their own small business . . . Essential reading . . . Here at last is a practical accessible handbook which will make sure your product or service gets the publicity it deserves.' *Great Ideas Newsletter (Business Innovations Research).* 'Explains how to put together a simple yet successful advertisement or brochure with the minimum of outside help . . . amply filled with examples and case studies.' *First Voice (National Federation of Self Employed and Small Businesses).*

£8.99, 176pp illus. 1 85703 213 6. Second edition.

Available from How To Books Ltd, Plymbridge House, Estover Road, Plymouth PL6 7PZ. Customer Services Tel: (01752) 202301. Fax: (01752) 202331.

Please add postage & packing (£1 UK, £2 Europe, £3 world airmail).

Credit card orders may be faxed or phoned.

6
Servicing Your Customers

Servicing your customers is not simply a case of sending them what they ordered and then forgetting about them. It is a way of ensuring that they are delighted with their purchase so that they will want to order from you again at some point in the future.

Many mail order operators ignore this vital point, and as a result they never manage to develop a solid base of satisfied customers. This makes it more difficult to succeed in the long term, because it is far more time-consuming and expensive to continue finding a constant supply of new customers than it is to encourage your past customers to shop with you again.

When a professional mail order operator services his customers properly, he has four main goals in mind:

1. to get the ordered product to the customer as quickly as possible
2. to get the ordered product to the customer as safely as possible
3. to ensure that his product is packaged and delivered in a professional manner
4. to try to make sure that the customer is delighted with his purchase.

This isn't as difficult as it may sound. To ensure that you service your customers to the best of your ability you need to develop a few simple habits and put a few simple strategies in place.

FULFILLING ORDERS

When orders come in, you should always ensure that they are fulfilled as **quickly and efficiently** as possible. Everyone knows how frustrating it can be to be kept waiting for something you have already paid for, and in the world of mail order this frustration is magnified somewhat, because your customers cannot see you at work and do not know why their order is taking so long. Your customers send their payment with their order, and they are entitled to expect that their order will be despatched just as soon as their payment clears.

Processing the order

To help you avoid keeping your customers waiting, you should consider working according to this simple system:

When orders arrive, check the details and the method of payment. Ensure that you have the name and full address of the customer, and that their payment is valid. If you receive an unsigned cheque or one which is incorrectly completed, now is the time when you want to identify that fact – not in a week or two.

Once you are satisfied that the paperwork is all present and correct, you should separate the order from the payment. Bank the cheques as quickly as possible and write the banking date on each order form. Then make a habit of fulfilling each order no more than ten working days (seven if possible) from the banking date. If a cheque bounces, your bank will notify you during this time, so no news is good news as far as this is concerned.

Packaging your product

When you come to prepare each order for despatch, try once again to think like a customer. Don't be mean with packaging. Instead, ensure that the product is packaged so that it has as much protection in transit as possible. Also, ensure that the package is as secure as possible.

The better your packaging, the less likely you are to get returns. This is because good packaging gives your customers the feeling that they are dealing with a true professional – and not with some cowboy who is only after their hard earned money. Again, this is another reason why you should avoid being mean with packaging materials. In the long run, poorly packaged products will greatly erode your chances of success.

Despatching your product

Sending the package itself can be done in a number of ways:

- by Royal Mail

- by courier

- by a parcel delivery firm.

Royal Mail

Small packages can often be sent very safely via the normal Royal Mail service. If the contents of the package are worth a lot of money, you might be wise to send it by Registered Post so that it is insured against loss or damage. If all you want is proof that the package has been received then Recorded Delivery will suffice.

Courier

Packages which need to be with your customer very quickly can be sent by courier. This is a more expensive way of sending products, but if speed is important to your customer, he will usually be prepared to cover this additional cost himself.

Parcel delivery firm

Large packages which are not desperately urgent can be sent by a parcel delivery firm. Ensure that the packaging is particularly protective if you use this method, as some firms are notoriously heavy handed. If in doubt, pad it out!

When you have despatched a product, write the date you sent it on the original order form. This will be useful in case a customer telephones you to say that he hasn't received it, and you can check to see if something might have gone awry. In most cases, the customer is simply being a little impatient and can be calmed with a few words of reassurance that their order is on its way.

Labelling the package

The better your customer feels when receiving your product, the more likely he is to order again in the future. Many mail order dealers make a habit of placing a label on all of their packages which read PRIORITY, CONFIDENTIAL, or something equally impressive. This makes the customer feel special when he receives the parcel, and the customer will often place another order just so that he has another opportunity to feel special in the future.

When an order has been fulfilled, you should place the order form in a suitable filing system. The way to file is totally up to you, but filing under client surname or date of order is usually most effective. As long as you can find a particular order quickly, any filing system will be suitable.

ADDING VALUE FOR CUSTOMERS

Before packaging each order you might want to think about adding extra value for your customer. This is simply giving your customer more than he or she expects, for no extra charge.

To many people, this sound ludicrous – to give material away for free. After all, mail order marketing is all about profit, isn't it?

Of course, mail order marketing is all about profit, but adding extra value for your customer is an excellent way of making your customer feel even more special. This encourages future orders and thus increases your profits over the long term.

Three ideas to start

There are many ways to add value to your customer's order. Here are just a few ideas:

- Enclose a free **booklet** which explains how to use your product to its best potential.

- Send a partial **refund**. If your customer paid £49 for a product, send him a cheque for £4.90 and announce that you have given him a further 10 per cent discount as a 'thank you for ordering'.

- Send a free **gift** which is related in some way to the product your customer has purchased.

Send any small gift which is related to the product your customer orders, and he will be delighted, especially if you attach an explanatory note which emphasises that this gift is totally free.

If you decide to send freebies with products, there is nothing wrong with raising the price of the product slightly to cover your additional costs. High street retailers do this all the time. One store may sell a pocket radio for £20, whilst another may be selling the same item for £25, but include a free pouch to keep it in. Chances are that both shops will sell an equal number of units, but the people who get the free radio pouch would – nine times out of ten – think that they received a better deal. Again, this is pure psychology, but nevertheless, amazingly effective.

There are other ways of adding value to your customers and making them feel special so that they are more inclined to order from you again. These will be discussed in a later chapter.

KEEPING RECORDS

Keeping accurate records need not be a meaningless chore as far as the mail order operator is concerned. Some records can actually help you to increase the overall efficiency and profitability of your business.

Keeping financial records

Apart from the records they need to keep for legal purposes, many mail order operators voluntarily keep monthly records of their income and expenditure for analysis purposes. Such a record can be kept in a simple cash book available from any high street stationery store. Simply use the left hand page to detail your total monthly income and the right hand page to detail your total monthly expenditure, as in the following example:

Month	Income	Month	Expenditure
April	£1,000	April	£300
May	£2,000	May	£400

Having such a record enables you to see how your business is progressing without having to wade through a mass of figures.

Advertising records

Keeping track of the amount of money you spend on advertising, compared with the amount of money which such advertising generates, is also very simple. For each advertisement you place, take a separate sheet of paper and note the date, cost and venue of the advertisement. As responses to this advertisement are received, make a note of them on the sheet of paper, as follows:

Date	Cost	Venue	Responses
01-04-96	£100	The Sunday Paper	32

As your business grows, you will probably place several different advertisements simultaneously, and it may therefore be difficult for you to decide which advert generated which response. To tackle this problem, you may wish to place a different 'code' in your address for each advertisement.

For example, if you place two advertisements, one in *The Sunday Paper* and one in *The Weekly Tabloid*, and your company is called XYZ Ltd, you could list your address as 'Dept SP1, XYZ Ltd' for the first advert and as 'Dept WT1, XYZ Ltd' for the second.

By doing this, you will know that any responses you receive which are addressed to Dept SP1 were generated from your advert in *The Sunday Paper*. At the same time, any responses you receive which are addressed to Dept WT1 were generated from your advert in *The Weekly Tabloid*.

CHARTING YOUR OPERATION

Using your records to help improve the performance of your mail order business is much easier if you draw up charts. Charts allow you to study the data contained in your records in a visual format, and thus see immediately how well (or poorly) your business is doing.

For example, here is a record of your income and expenditure for one month.

Month	Income	Month	Expenditure
April	£1,000	April	£300
May	£2,000	May	£400

It is clear that your business is improving, but by how much on a percentage basis? For example, if you wish to know how much gross income you are getting for every £100 you spend, you would divide £1,000 by 3 and £2,000 by 4 for April and May respectively. Let us place this data into a chart and take a look at the result (see Figure 9).

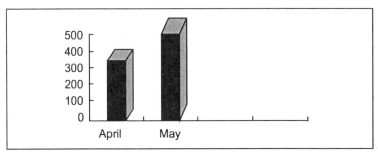

Fig. 9. Income received for every £100 expended.

Now that the data is presented in a visual format it is clear that the amount of income you received in proportion to the amount of money has risen quite markedly in the month of May. This is probably due to the fact that you are beginning to establish a reputation. People are seeing you advertise quite regularly and are therefore beginning to have more confidence in you as a legitimate company. As a consequence of this, more people are ordering from you and your income increases proportionately.

Let us examine another record: this time of advertising cost and the orders received as a result of such advertising:

Date	Advert and cost	Orders received
April 199X	Local £50	8 x £49 (£392 in value)
April 199X	National £500	40 x £49 (£1,960 in value)

As you can see, in the month of April, £50 was spent on an advertisement in a local newspaper, and this generated sales of £392. In the same month, a £500 advert in a national newspaper generated sales of £1,960.

At first glance it may look as though the national newspaper advert is more effective, because it has generated more income. But if you used a chart (Figure 10) to plot the number of responses per £50 of advertising, you would see a very different picture.

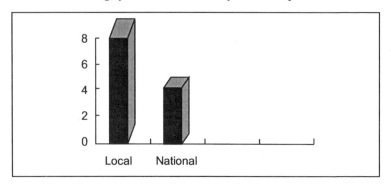

Fig. 10. Orders received per £50 advert cost.

It is now obvious that, pound for pound, the money spent on local advertising brings in twice the number of orders than national advertising. This information might lead you to concentrate your efforts on local marketing, and thus improve the overall profitability of your business.

Whilst charts are not likely to be of much use in the very early stages of your business, you may well find that they can be very good tools as your business grows. Obviously the examples in this chapter are given simply to indicate how the visualisation of data can help you to understand it better, but the message is clear: charts can be helpful.

Dealing with the orders you receive from customers and keeping records of your business are not the most glamorous aspects of mail order marketing, but they are two of the most important. Neglect them at your peril.

CHECKLIST

- Do you understand why giving quality service to your customers is vital?

- Do you understand why it is important to make your customers feel special?

- Can you see the point of giving added value to your customers?

- Do you know what records you need to keep to make your business effective?

- Do you know how to put simple record-keeping systems in place?

- Do you understand how charts can help you to make effective use of your records?

CASE STUDIES

Richard makes it special

Although Richard knows that the 'Stanford's Speech Accounts' package is great value, he realises that, to some people, paying £199 for a few computer discs and a manual might seem excessive. To appease such people, he makes a point of adding value by also sending his clients a book about the development and use of computer speech recognition systems in an accounting environment. He buys these books for just £2 each from a wholesaler, but since the cover price is £19.95, he is confident that his clients will be pleased with the gift.

Richard also pays attention to how he packages the product for despatch. He ensures that the contents are well protected, and places a label on each one which reads 'VERY URGENT – CONFIDENTIAL MATERIAL ENCLOSED'. Since the package is quite light, and the actual cost of the contents quite low, he sends it by Royal Mail's recorded delivery service.

Pauline charts her success

Even though her business is just a few weeks old, Pauline has placed quite a few classified advertisements in various magazines to generate enquiries about her knives. She has kept accurate records of how many responses she received from each advert, and after placing this data on a simple chart, she notices that her advertisements in three particular publications do very much better than the others.

Acting on this information, she reduces her advertising in the poorer publications and concentrates on using the ones which generate more response. The result is almost instantly recognisable. The number of enquiries she receives doubles within a month, and her business really begins to take off.

Alex polishes up his act

Alex decides that if he were a customer, he would like nothing better than receiving a surprise gift through the mail. He spends a day or two thinking of something which he can send to his customers to add a little extra value, but not damage his profits too much.

In the end he decides to send a compact disc cleaner with every order. The simple cleaner only costs his 50p, but it looks attractive and would doubtless be useful to his customers.

Within a week of sending out the free cleaner, he receives further orders from two customers who were impressed with their surprise gift. It suddenly dawns on Alex that if this is what can be expected in the future, adding value is a technique which he can use to increase his profits quite dramatically.

DISCUSSION POINTS

1. How could you add value for your customers?

2. Other than by sending a free gift, how else could you make them feel special when they receive their order?

3. How do you think keeping accurate records will help your business to succeed?

7
Increasing Customer Response

The amount of money you make in mail order is directly proportional to the response you get from your media and direct mail advertising. It follows that to make more money, you need to find a way of increasing customer response. That is what we will be talking about in this chapter.

Increasing customer response is not about increasing your level of advertising. If you mail 5,000 sales letters and get only 12 responses, spending money on another 5,000 mailshot is not going to make you particularly prosperous. Learning how to increase your response rate so that 250 people place an order from every 5,000 letters mailed is a much more effective solution.

Ways to increase responses
There are five major ways of increasing the response rate you get from your advertising efforts, and these are:

1. ensure that your advertising material is as good as it possibly could be
2. offer a free gift up-front
3. introduce the concept of a limited offer
4. give discounts
5. guarantee your products.

Used individually, each of these techniques will help to increase customer response. Use two or three together and your business will rocket.

REVISING YOUR ADVERTISING

If you want your advertising to be more effective, you need to make sure that it is as good as it possibly can be. The only way to determine if this is the case is to test several slightly different adverts and see which works best. Changes which professional mail order operators make to try and improve the 'pulling potential' of their advertising include:

Changing the headline of the sales letter or display advertisement
Sometimes all it takes to improve response is a more eye-catching headline. This encourages more people to read the text which follows and, subsequently, to place an order.

Revising the price of the product or service
Do not think that the only way to increase customer response by revising the price of your product is to reduce it. As we said in Chapter 2, raising your price is often equally effective. Try raising your price slightly before you try reducing it. The results may surprise you.

Revise the text itself
Make sure that the text of your advertisement doesn't ramble. Revise it completely if you think this is necessary, and make sure that it is snappy, emotive and a pleasure to read. The more your prospective clients are fascinated, excited or otherwise pleased to read your copy, the more likely they are to place an order.

OFFERING FREE GIFTS

We have already talked about how sending free gifts with an order adds value to your product and can help you to impress your customers. But why stop here? Why not mention your free gift up-front in your advertisement itself?

Most people, if they are in two minds about ordering from you, will err on the side of caution and let the opportunity pass them by. But including the promise of a free gift in your advertising is often the straw which breaks the camel's back as far as getting people to order from you is concerned. In many cases the offer will help you to receive orders from people who would have otherwise refrained from doing so.

As we said earlier, the type of free gift which you offer should be linked in some way to your primary product or service. It doesn't have to be much in terms of its cost to you, but it is important that you sell the benefits of this free gift in the same way as you sell the benefits of your main product.

Try to ensure that any free gift which you offer to potential customers is desirable. Tell the reader *why* he should want to take advantage of your special offer. Describe what the free gift will do for him. Tell him how it can help to improve the quality of his life or the performance of the main product.

Mail order companies which use this technique properly often find that a few people place orders just so that they can obtain the free gift! Now *that's* generating a response!

INTRODUCING LIMITED OFFERS

One of the most basic and powerful of human desires is to obtain something which is in short supply. Gold is deemed as being more valuable than iron simply because there is less of it available. Similarly, a **limited edition** of a product is perceived as being far more valuable than one which is freely available.

This basic desire for products and services which are in short supply can be exploited to amazing effect by a suitably knowledgeable mail order operator.

By announcing in your advertising materials that your product will be available for a limited period only, the level of interest amongst prospective customers will increase dramatically, and the number of orders you receive will follow suit.

One thing which you should bear in mind when announcing limited offers is that they must be genuine. Do not assume that you can announce a limited offer and let it go on forever.

If you do not wish to limit the availability of your actual product, you could offer it at a reduced price for a limited period. Let us imagine that you had originally intended to sell a product for £39. You can exploit the 'limited offer' desire by stating that your product is available for £39 for a limited period only, and that when the period is over, you will raise the price to (say) £49.

The advantage of doing this is that you will get a much better response when the product is offered at £39 for a limited period than if no limited period was announced.

GIVING DISCOUNTS

Let's imagine that you have offered a product for £39 for a limited period only. That limited period is now over and the price of your product has increased to £49. Now how do you continue to get a good response from prospective customers?

The answer is to offer a discount for a fast response! Announce that anyone who orders within a certain length of time will be eligible for a £10 price reduction.

This tactic allows you to continue selling your product for £39 as long as your customers order quickly. If they are slow then they must pay the full £49.

Another technique which many mail order operators use is to set the 'recommended retail price' with the knowledge that they will reduce this by £10 or so to make a good advertising deal. Thus, offering a product which has a rrp of £49 for just £39 sounds a lot more attractive than just saying £39. Again, this is a tactic which plays on basic human emotions, and is therefore very effective.

GUARANTEEING YOUR PRODUCTS

When anyone makes a purchase by mail order, they are entitled to return the product within seven days and ask for a full refund of their money. This statutory guarantee is not mentioned by many newcomers to mail order because they fear that it will encourage people to return their products and profits will fall. In fact the contrary is usually true.

When people are offered a guarantee, they are far less likely to hesitate about making a purchase than otherwise. Thus customer response increases dramatically.

Furthermore, you are not offering any more than your customer is legally entitled to anyway, so you do not lose out one iota. Of course, you will get people returning your products occasionally, but if you have ensured that your product is fit for the purpose it is intended for, these will normally be the exception rather than the rule.

The most successful mail order operators use guarantees to even greater effect. Instead of saying 'Seven day money-back guarantee' they extend the statutory guarantee to a month, three months, a year and sometimes even longer.

This technique is not as silly as it might first appear. Human nature being what it is, customers are likely to forget about the guarantee when they receive the product and begin using it. But without that guarantee, they might not have purchased in the first place. Thus a long guarantee period will greatly increase the response you get from your advertising, but actual returns will still be very small as a proportion of your total sales.

Guarantees show the customer that you have faith in your product. They show that you are willing to 'put your money where your mouth is'. Consequently, the customer begins to have faith in you and places an order.

Increasing the bottom line

In conclusion, the way to increase the response to your advertising efforts is not to immediately do more of it, but to first make your advertising more effective. The tools you have studied in this chapter are ones which the most successful mail order operators use on a regular basis. And professionals being what they are, they only use them because they help to increase the bottom line. Guaranteed!

CHECKLIST

- Do you understand why increasing customer response is important?

- Is your headline as attention-grabbing as possible?

- Is your advertising text the best you can make it?

- Do you understand how offering free gifts can help to increase response?

- Do you understand how a limited offer can help to increase response?

- Have you given a guarantee in your advertisement text?

- Do you know how to give discounts without reducing your profit?

- Do you now realise how simple it is to increase response?

CASE STUDIES

Richard makes himself accountable

'Use it for 30 days, and if you don't like it, receive your money back!'

These are the words which Richard adds to his advertising materials in order to increase response. He knows that once his clients begin using the 'Stanford's Speech Accounts' package, they will wonder how they managed to live without it. The guarantee will (hopefully) encourage people to try the product in the first place.

Of course, Richard expects that one or two people will return the product, but this might have happened anyway. Using the guarantee, sales should increase and more than make up for any additional refunds he has to make in the future.

Pauline sells the obvious

One of the major selling points of 'The Sherring Swiss Blade Set' is that the knives are guaranteed for ten years. Pauline has already mentioned this in her sales literature, but now she thinks that she might try to emphasise this fact.

Pauline revises her sales letter so that the guarantee is presented in a boxed area just before the order form. She emphasises the quality of her product and really goes to town on selling the guarantee as a major benefit to the customer. This should eradicate any doubts the reader has about the quality of the knives, and orders should subsequently increase.

Alex gives a discount

Alex doesn't think that his compact disc cleaner – effective though it is – would be a particularly big incentive for prospective customers. So instead he decides to raise the recommended retail price of his 'Treble Clef Tutorials' from £29.99 to £39.99, then adds a line to his sales literature which reads,

ORDER WITHIN 14 DAYS AND RECEIVE
£10 DISCOUNT!

The saving looks huge, and should encourage readers not only to order, but to order quickly.

DISCUSSION POINTS

1. How might you be able to use two or more of the techniques in this chapter at the same time?

2. Why do you think some people are hesitant about ordering goods by mail order?

3. How can you change your advertising materials to reassure these hesitant people?

8
Exploiting Back End Marketing

When you advertise your products or services in order to attract potential customers to buy them from you, you are using what is known as 'front end' marketing. **'Back end' marketing** is the name given to the effort of encouraging new customers to place another order. The idea is that you send additional sales-related literature to the customer when you fulfil their first order, and thus take a 'piggy back' ride on an existing sale.

Back end marketing is one of the most valuable strategies a mail order operator has at his disposal, but surprisingly, many people overlook it.

The tendency to be satisfied with having made a sale at all is probably what stops most operators from using back end marketing on a regular basis, but ignorance is no excuse.

Making the most of the customer's satisfaction

If you do your job properly, then when your customer receives his order he will:

- be pleased at how quickly his order was fulfilled

- be pleasantly surprised that he got more than he expected (added value)

- feel special.

This being the case, what better time is there to ask your customer to make another purchase? After all, if his first purchase made him feel so good, and your product is genuinely useful, why shouldn't he order again?

Of course, back end marketing is more than just sending another sales letter with the product – this could give the impression that you are out to get all that you can. To be efficient, a back end marketing piece must make the customer feel even more special, and there are several ways of doing this.

REINFORCING THE BENEFITS

By the time your customer receives his order, chances are that the emotion which initially compelled him to make a purchase from you has all but disappeared. The first step in creating an effective back end marketing piece is therefore to reinforce the benefits of your product so that he experiences that emotional excitement all over again.

Open your letter by thanking your customer for his order, then take a few of the most powerful paragraphs of your sales letter and remind him of what he has purchased. 'Not just a computer programme, but a method of saving both time and money....'

When you are confident that the opening of your letter has sufficiently reinforced the benefits of your product, you can introduce the main part of your message, the crux of which will be, 'We know you'll love what you ordered, so here's something else you might be interested in....'

RECOMMENDING RELATED PRODUCTS

The easiest way to make back end marketing pay is to recommend another **related product**. For example, if you are selling a manual which teaches people how to restore and maintain classic cars, you may wish to offer your customers a 'restoration and maintenance kit' containing paints, polishes, and so on, which they would need to purchase anyway if they wish to follow the advice in the manual.

Again the rules for selling this back end product are exactly the same as when you created text to sell your primary product. You need to sell the features and benefits of your product in an exciting, emotive manner, and make your offer as difficult to refuse as possible by using one or more of the strategies given in the last chapter.

COLLABORATING WITH OTHER COMPANIES

If you do not have access to a related product, and cannot obtain one, think about collaborating with another company which offers products that are in some way related to yours.

The basic idea is that you approach a company and offer to act as an agent for their product. Point out that you operate a mail order business and are willing to offer their product to your existing customers and split profits on a 50-50 basis.

To some people, collaborating with other companies may seem self-defeating – after all, why should you help another company to increase its profits?

If you are one of these people then you must bear in mind that 50 per cent of something is better than 100 per cent of nothing. Of course, it would be far better to obtain your own secondary product to sell via back end marketing, but if that is not possible, the obvious next best thing is to increase your profit by selling the product of another company.

Many companies are more open to this sort of deal than you might expect. They have nothing to lose from allowing you to market their products, and they will receive a welcome increase in profits for doing absolutely nothing.

ASKING FOR REFERRALS

Selling additional products or services on the back end of an existing sale is not the only way to increase your profits. Another useful strategy is to simply ask your client for a few referrals. These are names and addresses of friends or family who your customer thinks may also have an interest in your products and services.

Although this strategy will not result in an immediate increase in orders and profitability, it is an excellent way to **increase your customer base**. And remember, the wider your customer base, the better your chances of building a successful mail order business which is capable of giving you the financial security you have always wanted.

Of course, it should go without saying that your customers will seldom want to give referrals out of the goodness of their heart. For this strategy to be effective, you need to offer something in return for referrals.

Rewarding your customers

The easiest way of rewarding your customers who give you referrals is to offer them a free gift or discount voucher for every referral they give you which is converted to a sale. This encourages your customer to give as many referrals as possible, and also means that you do not have to give anything away unless at least one of those referrals is converted into a profitable sale.

The power of referrals can be immense. If just two of your customers each refer two people who become customers, and they do the same, the net result is that you will have added twelve new customers to your client base! And if these twelve new customers each help you to make a sale to two other people, you will increase your base by another 24 customers!

Obtaining referrals, as we have already said, can be a slow process, but the potential they give the mail order business is incredible.

WINNING REPEAT ORDERS

If your product is consumable and will need to be replaced in the future then you might be tempted to think that your back end marketing will take care of itself. After all, if they need more of the same, they will order from you, right?

Don't bet on it. If your customers can get the same or a similar product elsewhere then many of them will – if only to see what your competitors are like.

To guard against this, invite the customer to place future repeat business with you and enjoy a discount, additional free gift or other incentive. This will encourage customer loyalty, and ensure that your profits don't take a nose-dive in the future.

To summarise, back end marketing is an amazing method of increasing your profits by taking a 'piggy-back ride' on the back of an existing sale. It is one of the most effective ways of increasing your overall profitability, and using it will ensure that your business stands the best possible chance of success.

CHECKLIST

- Do you understand the concept of back end marketing?

- Can you see the advantages of using back end marketing strategies?

- Does your primary product have the potential for repeat business?

- If not, could you obtain and market a related product?

- If not, are you willing to collaborate with another company?

- Do you understand how powerful asking for referrals can be?

CASE STUDIES

Richard develops a portable deal

Since many accountants use portable or laptop computers between the office and home, Richard spends a few months developing a more basic version of the 'Stanford's Speech Accounts' package especially for these computers. He obtains a bulk purchase of small portable microphones and creates a 'Stanford's Mini Speech Accounts' package. He offers this to anyone who purchases his primary product for just £149, but offers a discount of 33 per cent if they order within 21 days.

Within a month of introducing this back end product, Richard's profits increase dramatically. What's more, some clients who do not yet have portable computers have telephoned him to ask if he sells these too. Richard replies that he doesn't at the moment, but that he's working on the idea and will contact them shortly....

Pauline makes her money in blocks

The natural back end product as far as Pauline is concerned is a professional standard knife-block. She spends several weeks finding a manufacturer of a quality, sold wooden block which will store her knives safely and neatly.

In her back end literature Pauline reminds her clients of the benefits her knives give – mainly of their sharpness and quality. She builds on this by suggesting that the knives should be taken care of properly if her customers want to get the best performance out of them, and recommends the 'Sherring Swiss Blade Block' as a suitable solution.

Like Richard, Pauline experiences a healthy increase in profitability, and she receives several letters complimenting her on the quality of her products and service.

Alex asks for referrals

Alex feels that the best way for him to profit from back end marketing is to ask for referrals from satisfied customers. To encourage these, he offers a £5 discount voucher which can be redeemed against any future order for every referral who subsequently becomes a customer. If a customer refers five or more people at any one time, a £6 discount is offered for each conversion.

The referrals take quite a while to arrive, and not everyone bothers to send any. Those who do, however, more often than not send five or more names in order to try and claim a greater discount against their future orders.

This result pleases Alex, for not only does it help him to create a larger customer base, it also indicates that many of his existing customers would be happy to order from him again. After all, if they weren't, why should they be interested in trying to obtain discount vouchers?

Although the growth of his business is a little slower than that experienced by Richard and Pauline, because it takes longer to turn referrals into sales, the growth does come. And as he gets more customers, he gets more referrals. Pretty soon it occurs to Alex that a snowball effect has started to take place and that his business is automatically cruising towards the success he wants.

DISCUSSION POINTS

1. How have companies tried to use back end marketing techniques on you?

2. Were these techniques effective, and if so, why?

3. How would you try to improve these techniques in your own business?

9
Working as a Professional

Although mail order marketing is an excellent opportunity for the entrepreneurial spirit, like any business, it is highly competitive. Working in an **honest** and **professional** manner will help to ensure that your business is still operational long after the 'cowboys' and 'con-men' have hit the dust.

LIVING THE IMAGE

It is not enough simply to exude an image of professionalism – it is vital that you live the image too. Begin to think, speak and act like a professional and that is what you will become. Treat your mail order business as a game or hobby and you are handicapping yourself.

There are three main qualities of professionalism which, if you develop them, will help you achieve your goals and dreams. These qualities are:

- self-discipline
- optimism
- enthusiasm.

Be self-disciplined

Because you are self-employed, what you do with your working day is entirely up to you. You can work when you want, where you want, in any manner you want. Although these are tremendous benefits when used wisely, they can also work against you.

Arrange your working week as you want it, but be sure to be self-disciplined and actually work at the appropriate times. As the saying goes, 'plan your work, and work your plan'. This is a major key to success in all walks of life.

One thing which you must definitely guard against is **procrastination**, or putting off work which you know should be done. This is an extremely bad habit to develop and will eventually ruin any chance of success you would otherwise have.

Be optimistic

Success is always easier to achieve if you develop and maintain a **positive mental attitude**. Expect success and that is what you will get. Expect failure and that too is inevitable. This isn't a trite piece of self-help psychobabble – it is a very real concept which almost all successful business people live by. Do the same and you too will succeed. Remember, 'whether you believe you can, or whether you believe you can't – you're right!'

Be enthusiastic

If you are not enthusiastic about your business and the products and services which you offer, how can you expect anyone else to be? If you approach your business with **energy, enthusiasm** and a real **belief** in the benefits which your products or services can give others, this enthusiasm will come across in your sales literature and help you to vastly increase your income.

DEALING WITH REGULATORY BODIES

As you work as a professional, you will have to deal with regulatory bodies at some point or another. A regulatory body is simply an organisation which exists to protect the rights of consumers and ensure that 'cowboys' and 'con-men' are eradicated as quickly as possible.

There are many different types of regulatory bodies, each of which serves a different purpose. As far as the mail order world is concerned, the three main ones are:

- Data Protection Registrar
- Advertising Standards Authority (ASA)
- Mail Order Protection Scheme (MOPS).

The Data Protection Registrar

If for any reason you intend to keep a mailing list of previous customers and store these details on computer, you must first of all register with this regulatory body. Consumers have a legal right to know what information is being stored about them and why. They also have a right to request that you do not pass on their names to other companies, or that you do not send unsolicited mailings to them in the future. It is your duty to contact the registrar and work within the law as far as this is concerned.

The Advertising Standards Authority

This regulatory body exists to ensure that all claims made in advertisements are true, honest and reliable. As well as protecting consumers from companies which purposely seek to mislead people through their advertising, the body also helps to make sure that all companies are advertising within the same strict guidelines. As far as you are concerned, this means that you can compete with other companies on an equal footing, confident in the knowledge that all of you are playing by the same basic rules.

If you are ever unsure as to whether your advertising materials are acceptable, you can always contact the ASA and receive free advice. This will help you to avoid any possible problems which could crop up later.

MOPS

The Mail Order Protection Scheme, or MOPS, was set up to protect customers in the event of a mail order purchase being unfulfilled due to a company going out of business. Membership is voluntary, but without it you will not be able to sell off the page in national newspapers.

Membership fees are in proportion to the amount of money you expect to spend on advertising in any given year, and are revised annually.

Apart from the fact that being a member of MOPS is essential if you want to sell off the page in national newspapers, membership can also increase your profits in other media. This is because being a member gives the public more confidence in your legitimacy and honesty. Hence the number of orders you receive increases – and so does your overall profitability.

Dealing with regulatory bodies

The key to having good working relationships with regulatory bodies is to abide by their rules and keep your nose clean. Work as a professional, with honesty and integrity, and you should never run into any trouble. On the contrary, your chances of success are vastly increased if you abide by the rules of the game.

USING SPECIALISTS

There are specialists who can help you in all areas of your business. Some are more essential than others, but this will depend on your trading status, and the size of your business.

Using accountants

The job of an accountant is to prepare your accounts for the Inland Revenue and Companies House if you are trading as a limited company. Whilst, as a sole trader, you can prepare your own accounts for tax purposes, many people prefer to let a qualified accountant take care of this so that they are free to do what they do best – make money by mail order.

If you are a sole trader and are fairly knowledgeable about how to keep your financial records in good order, then you may not want to use the services of an accountant. If, on the other hand, you are trading as a limited company, or have little knowledge of book-keeping and preparing accounts for tax self-assessment, an accountant will be a necessary expense.

Like most specialists, accountants usually charge according to how much work they have to do on your behalf. If they need to wet-nurse you through every stage of recording your financial transactions, then they will charge more than if all they need to do is take up-to-date records and prepare a set of accounts from them.

If you would like to use an accountant, but do not want to pay through the nose for a high level of service, you could teach yourself book-keeping and make his job easier. Suitable resources for doing this can be found in the Further Reading section at the end of this book.

Using consultants

Mail order consultants come in all shapes and sizes. All exist to help your business grow and become more profitable.

Some consultants specialise in helping you to create and obtain suitable mail order products. Others, like myself, help people to create effective advertising materials by using professional copy-writing techniques and a knowledge of consumer psychology.

The fees which consultants charge vary from reasonable to extortionate. Whilst it is usually true that 'you get what you pay for', a newcomer to the world of mail order would be better off trying to use consultants whose fees are in the low to medium range, or better still – do without them until their business grows into something substantial.

Using solicitors

Most small mail order companies can manage perfectly well without having to use the services of a solicitor, but as your business grows, you may find that a solicitor is a useful specialist to call upon. Solicitors can draw up contracts for collaborations between companies, help you to change your trading status, help you to protect a genuinely original product and provide many other valuable legal services.

Dealing with specialists

When dealing with any kind of specialist, you should make it clear at your initial meeting exactly what you are looking for. Given a clear goal, the specialist should then be able to estimate how much work will be involved and therefore give you a quote as to how much his services will cost.

Remember that the specialist is working for you, and not the other way around. By all means take qualified advice, but do not think that you are giving up a part of your business to someone else. When all is said and done, your business is your responsibility, and that of no one else.

HIRING EMPLOYEES

As your business grows, the number of orders you need to fulfil will naturally increase. Eventually you may want to employ someone to help you run your business; either to help you keep up with demand or to give you more free time.

You could employ friends or family, or you could advertise in a local newspaper in order to find someone suitable. Whichever method you use, there are certain **legal obligations** which you should at least be aware of before you employ someone.

As an employer, you will be required to pay tax and national insurance contributions on behalf of your employee. You must ensure that their working environment complies with health and safety regulations, and that you have adequate insurance to cover your liability as an employer. Because legislation pertaining to employees is changing constantly, you would be wise to obtain professional advice before making a firm offer of employment to anyone.

A useful alternative

If hiring employees is not something that you would like to get involved in, you can hire what is known as a **fulfilment house** to handle everything from processing your orders to preparing and despatching products accordingly.

The main advantage of using a fulfilment house is that you can hire their services as and when you need them. There is no contract of employment to adhere to and no need for any of the red tape which is necessary when employing a member of staff. Because of this, many mail order marketing businesses work with a minimum of staff and use fulfilment houses during particularly busy times.

Having employees or using a fulfilment house will allow you to take a less active role in your business. Eventually, you may, if you wish, act simply as the 'ideas man' and get your staff to take the practical steps necessary to turn these ideas into profit. At this point, the world is your oyster, and you will have joined the ranks of the professional mail order marketeer, who doesn't find it necessary to work long 'rat-race' hours in order to succeed.

CHANGING YOUR TRADING STATUS

Once your business has evolved into a dynamic, cash-rich organisation, you may find that it is either necessary or desirable to change your trading status from that of a sole trader to becoming the director of your own limited company. At this point you may wish to take the advice of a solicitor to guide you on your way, but the actual change of trading status is not complicated.

Companies House and your solicitor will be able to guide you through the necessary red tape to forming your own limited company, and further sources of help are given in the Further Reading section at the end of this book.

Working as a professional will enable you to succeed far beyond your previous expectations. As the captain at the helm of a business with unlimited potential, you will be on course to realise your goals and ambitions. You will be free of the nine-to-five rat race once and for all.

CHECKLIST

- Are you willing to discipline yourself?

- Do you understand what it means to 'plan your work and work your plan'?

- Are you committed to developing a positive mental attitude?

- Are you enthusiastic about running your own mail order marketing business?

- Do you understand the role of regulatory bodies?

- Do you understand how specialists may be able to help you in the future?

CASE STUDIES

Richard works his plan

Richard finds that he is comfortable setting himself the same nine-to-five hours which he used to work as an employee. He treats his mail order business as seriously as he treated his employed position, and makes sure that he is always at his desk right on time. He sets himself goals and works hard to achieve them, then closes the door of his small study (which used to be the spare bedroom) at 5pm every Friday and forgets about work until the following week.

Richard knows that he can work when he wants and that no one is forcing him to keep such strict hours, but finds that the habit of a lifetime is hard to break. Besides, in a few years he hopes to have a small staff of people to take over his position so that he can enjoy more golf. If it takes a few years of hard work and regular hours to achieve that goal, he's happy to pay the price.

Pauline works around the family

One of the main things that attracted Pauline to running her own mail order business was the fact that she could fit work around her family. She works for a few hours each afternoon and occasionally in the evenings. Mail order has given her the opportunity of earning a full-time income whilst working part-time hours, and this suits her down to the ground.

Pauline is fast developing a good head for business and her marketing skills and aptitude are increasing on a daily basis. Her husband has taken a keen interest in her mail order business and has even discussed resigning from his employed position and going into partnership with her.

Alex plays it by ear

Alex takes full advantage of being able to work as and when he likes. At the beginning of each week he checks when his private tutorials are scheduled to take place and plans to work around those. However, he often has to revise his plan to make room for extra tutorials, and in this sense he plays it by ear as far as his working hours are concerned.

That said, Alex ensures that he does whatever it takes to get things done in an orderly and professional manner. He already has an accountant, so he doesn't have to worry too much about finding the time to keep more than basic financial records. A little book-keeping is all that is necessary to keep his financial affairs in order.

The flexibility of mail order allows Alex to continue servicing his current music students, whilst at the same time develop a very welcome additional income – one which he thinks will eventually provide him with financial security so that he can retire from tutoring altogether.

DISCUSSION POINTS

1. What does 'working as a professional' mean to you?

2. How can working as a professional help you to succeed?

3. How might using specialists enable you to increase your income?

10
Expanding Your Business

If you want to assure your survival and success in the world of mail order marketing, you must make a habit of pushing beyond the boundaries you have become used to. Never get into the habit of being satisfied with where you are. Never allow yourself to be content with your status, your income or your achievements. In all areas of life, the people who succeed the most are the people who constantly set themselves new goals and push themselves to break their own personal records of achievement.

There are five major ways in which you can actively work to expand your business. These are:

1. establish your reputation

2. obtain media coverage

3. increase your customer base

4. expand your trading horizons

5. sell your experience.

ESTABLISHING YOUR REPUTATION

It is said that, in Hollywood, an actor is only as good as his last movie. Similarly, in the business world, a mail order marketing company is only as good as its current reputation. If you develop a bad reputation, your sales will decline rapidly. If, on the other hand, you establish a good reputation, your sales will increase.

One of the best ways of establishing a good reputation is to let your **satisfied customers** speak on your behalf. If a customer sends you a complimentary letter of thanks for your product or service, contact the client and ask for permission to use an excerpt of his

97

MONEY LISTENS AS WELL AS TALKS!

Thanks to the enterprising efforts of Richard Stanford, a computer programmer, accountants may soon discover that money listens as well as talks!

Mr Stanford, of Software By Mail, has created a computer accountancy program called 'Stanford's Speech Accounts' which is capable of obeying the spoken commands of its user. This is achieved by using a clever speech recognition process, and Mr Stanford claims that it will help the average accountant save almost three working days each year, thus increasing productivity and profits.

'Stanford's Speech Accounts' is only available by mail order and is priced at a remarkably competitive £199 including postage and packaging costs.

For further details contact Richard Stanford on 01234 567890.

Fig. 11. An example press release.

testimonial in your advertising materials. This will be granted by most customers, particularly if there is a discount voucher or small gift offered in return.

What you should **never** do is 'engineer' testimonials from customers. By all means you should make it clear that you welcome feedback, but do not be seen to offer incentives for compliments. That's a dirty trick which, if it ever comes to light, will shatter any reputation for honesty you have worked so hard to develop.

Another thing you need to keep in mind is that the public have a right to examine any testimonials you use in your advertising. For this reason you should ensure that any testimonial you use is signed and dated by the customer, and that the customer is happy to be approached for verification if necessary.

That said, using testimonials is a very effective way of establishing your reputation for honesty, integrity and professionalism. When a client says something good about your company and its wares, prospective clients are given confidence in you, and are therefore more likely to place an order.

OBTAINING MEDIA COVERAGE

It is a testimony to the power of the media that people belive almost everything they read in newspapers, hear on the radio or see on television. The fact is that information conveyed by the media is seen to be more trustworthy and reliable than if the same information had been conveyed by some other means. It follows that if you can get the media to say something nice about you, you will experience a great increase in sales and profits.

Drafting effective press releases

The easiest way to get media coverage is to write a **press release** and send it to as many media companies as possible. A press release is simply a one or two page article about your company, products and services, written in the third person (see Figure 11). In order for it to be effective, it should:

● have an interesting headline

● be newsworthy

● be typed double-spaced on standard A4 bond paper

- be no more than two sides long

- have a contact name and number at the end.

If you are interested in using press releases as a way of obtaining valuable media coverage then I strongly recommend that you study a book called *How to Write a Press Release* by Peter Bartram. Full details of this title can be found in the Further Reading section at the end of this book.

EXPANDING YOUR CLIENT BASE

Customers are the lifeblood of your business, and it is vital that you expand your client base as far as possible as quickly as possible in order to achieve rapid growth and success. In Chapter 7 we discussed ways of increasing customer response, but here we are talking about how you can reach more people in the first place.

If, after several months of being in business, you come to enjoy a certain amount of success by mailing 5,000 sales letters per month, do not allow yourself to become satisfied with this result. Reinvest a proportion of your profits and begin sending 10,000 letters a month. When that begins to feel comfortable, increase your mailings to 20,000 per month, and so on.

The net result of this constant expansion is that your business will grow at an astonishing rate, and it won't be long before you are either employing staff or using fulfilment houses on a regular basis. When this happens, congratulate yourself – you will be living your dream!

TRADING INTERNATIONALLY

One of the greatest things about mail order is that you are not restricted to selling products and services solely within your own locality. Trading internationally is not much more complicated than trading nationally.

Before you begin to trade internationally, you *must* research the foreign markets and ensure that there is a demand for your product or services. You must also be absolutely certain that when you send your product or service abroad, it will be fit to be used for its intended purpose. This is obviously no problem if you are selling jewellery or some other ornamental product, but if you deal in electrical equipment or factual 'how to' books, you need to be certain that they will be useful to foreign purchasers.

You should also set in place systems to deal with foreign currency payments, the international despatch of products and, if necessary, the translation of your sales literature.

Although the idea of trading internationally will appeal to some readers, others will not be so interested. If this is the case with you then do not feel that selling your products and services globally is an essential ingredient to expanding your business. The fact is that the British mail order market alone is more than big enough to give you a very real chance of becoming financially independent.

SELLING YOUR EXPERIENCE

The final strategy for expanding your business is to become something of a 'personality'. As your experience of the mail order world grows, you may wish to help others learn from your successes and failures and at the same time raise your public profile.

There are four main ways in which you can sell your experience. Depending on your abilities and personal preferences, you could:

- write articles for magazines and newspapers

- write a book

- organise and speak at seminars

- become a mail order consultant.

These activities will allow you to bring more attention to your business and at the same time profit as a 'personality'. If you can leave the actual running of your company in the hands of a capable staff or fulfilment house then becoming a full-time expert may pay big dividends.

Once you begin operating as an expert, you will find that you enter a circle of success. Whenever you sell your experience, you take a step further into the public eye. As your fame grows, your business will also grow. And as your business grows, you will find that you are in greater demand as a personality.

Examples of traditional business people who have successfully stepped into this 'circle of success' are Richard Branson, Anita Roddick and Victor Kiam, to name just a few. Of course, all of these people continue to work very hard as the captains of their business organisations, but by selling their experience and being willing to share the stories of their successes and failures, their businesses have expanded dramatically.

I'm not necessarily saying that selling your experience will make you the next Richard Branson – not everyone wants this. What I am saying is that selling your experience can only help to expand your business. As your business expands, so will the size of your bank account!

CHECKLIST

- Do you understand why expanding your business is so important?

- Do you realise the importance of establishing a reputation?

- Do you know how a press release can help you obtain media coverage?

- Do you understand how to expand your client base?

- Can you see how selling your experience can help your business grow?

CASE STUDIES

Richard builds a business empire

In less than a year, Richard has gone from being a bored nine-to-five professional to the owner of a thriving mail order marketing business. After the success of his two computer packages, 'Stanford's Speech Accounts' and 'Stanford's Mini Speech Accounts', Richard begins marketing portable computers and other executive tools. He uses press releases on a regular basis and although not all have been used, some have been dramatically successful. His local radio station mentioned his 'Stanford's Speech Accounts' package in their lunchtime bulletin and this created a massive surge of interest which culminated in a feature in the local newspaper.

Richard has seen the potential of his business and is now committed to building his very own empire. Following his accountant's advice, he has changed his trading status and is now the proud director of Stanford Software Ltd. His company may not grow to rival the computer giants, but he is certain that he will be able to retire very comfortably in less than ten years.

Pauline takes on a partner

Although her success is not as dramatic as that experienced by Richard Stanford, Pauline's business steadily grows to the point where her husband cannot resist getting involved. He resigns from his job and helps to build the business as a partner. Within two years they expand their product line to include electrical catering equipment and manage to secure several lucrative contracts with major manufacturers as approved mail order retailers. Needless to say, they now stock their products in a local warehouse instead of their garage!

Pauline and her husband have no ambition to conquer the world, but they do realise the importance of self-promotion and publicity. To this end, Pauline writes articles for catering magazines on a regular basis, and has become something of an expert in her chosen field. What's more, she still has the pleasure of working flexible hours and spending time with her family.

Alex goes Stateside

As the months pass, Alex finds that the demand for personal music tuition steadily declines. Fortunately, his mail order business quickly establishes itself and provides him with a very comfortable level of income, so much so that he decides to leave his business in the capable hands of a professional fulfilment house whilst he has a three month vacation in America.

But the mail order itch has well and truly grabbed Alex and relaxing abroad is not easy. He begins to investigate the mail order market in the USA and discovers to his great delight that there appears to be a niche in the market for his products.

Six months later, Alex is receiving orders from California, Texas and Florida. It seems that Treble Clef Ltd is as popular Stateside as it is here at home.

DISCUSSION POINTS

1. How can expanding your business help you achieve your goals?

2. How might a press release help you obtain media coverage for your product?

3. How could you sell your experience in your locality and raise the public profile of both yourself and your business?

Glossary

Back end marketing. Encouraging an existing customer to place a further order by enclosing additional sales literature when you despatch their product.

Body copy. The main text of your sales letter which describes the features and benefits of your product.

Classified advertisments. Small text-only advertisements used to generate requests for more detailed product information. Usually used as part of the two step advertising strategy.

Direct mail. The sending of sales literature and order forms directly to potential customers.

Display advertisements. Media advertisements (usually quite large) which can contain text, illustrations and a clip-coupon order form if required.

Established market. The sector of the market made up of products that have a proven record of success.

Fad market. The sector of the market made up of novelty and fad items, which usually have limited appeal and life-span.

Fulfilment. The act of fulfiling orders received from customers.

Headline. The opening sentence of a sales letter or display advertisement. The headline is designed to attract attention and encourage readers to study the text which follows.

Mailing list. A list of potential customers for use with the direct mail advertising strategy.

Marketing plan. A document which contains the main objectives and strategies of a mail order marketing business.

Referrals. The names of potential customers given by existing customers. Referrals are used to increase the customer base of a mail order marketing operator.

Typesetting. The design and arrangement of text and illustrations on paper in preparation for printing.

USP. The abbreviation for Unique Selling Proposition. A unique quality which sets one product apart from another.

Useful Addresses

REGULATORY BODIES

Advertising Standards Authority, Brook House, 2–16 Torrington Place, London WC1E 7HN. Tel: (0171) 580 5555.

Data Protection Registrar, Wycliffe House, Water Lane, Wilmslow, Cheshire SK9 5AF. Tel: Wilmslow 535777.

Mail Order Protection Scheme, 16 Took's Court, London EC4A 1LB. Tel: (0171) 405 6806.

Direct Mail Services Standards Board, 26 Eccleston Street, London SW1W 9PY. Tel: (0171) 824 8651.

LIST MANAGEMENT AND BROKERAGE

Hilite Direct Marketing Services, Ash House, Ash Road, Longfield, Kent DA3 8SA.

Chartsearch plc, Charles House, Charles Square, London N1 6HT. Tel: (0171) 417 0700.

MAIL ORDER CONSULTANTS AND COPYWRITERS

Ian Bruce, Unit 2, Gate House, Framfield, East Sussex TN22 5RS.

Hilite Direct Marketing Sercvices, Ash House, Ash Road, Longfield, Kent DA3 8SA.

GENERAL

Companies House, Crown Way, Maindy, Cardiff CF4 3UZ.

Further Reading

How to Do Your Own Advertising, Michael Bennie (How To Books).
How to Do Your Own PR, Ian Phillipson (How To Books).
How to Keep Business Accounts, Peter Taylor (How To Books).
How to Write a Press Release, Peter Bartram (How To Books).
Profit Through the Post, Alison Cork (Piatkus 1994).
Selling by Direct Mail, John W Graham and Susan K Jones (Piatkus 1988).

Index

accountants, 21, 92
adding value, 34, 70-71
advertisements, 42-43, 59-67
Advertising Standards Author-
    ity, 91
answering machines, 20

back end marketing, 83-88
banks, 22
billboards, 65
body copy, 52
broadcast media, 63
business name, 19

charts, 73-75
classified advertisements, 59-60
cold advertising words, 49, 51
collaborating, 84-85
competitors, 39
consultants, 92
copywriters, 92
customer stereotypes, 31-32

Data Protection Registrar, 90
deal, getting the best, 65
direct mail, 42, 46-58
discounts, 79-80
display advertisements, 60-63

employees, 93-94
emotion, 48-49
envelopes, 55

established markets, 28-29
expansion, 97-103

fad markets, 29-30
free gifts, 71, 78-79
fulfilment, 68-70

guarantees, 80

headlines, 47-48
hot advertising words, 49-50

ideas, generating, 30-31
illustrations, 61-62
image, 19-20, 89-90
income tax, 22
insurance, 22-23
Internet, 65

limited companies, 21
limited offers, 79
locating customers, 37-38

mailing lists, 53
market analysis, 27-30
marketing plan, 37-45
marketing strategies, 41-43
MOPS, 91

National Insurance, 22
new markets, 30
niche, identifying a, 31-32

offer
  packaging, 53, 55
  testing, 55-56
one step advertising, 42
orders, processing, 68-70

press release, 98-100
print media, 1, 42-43
product
  despatching, 69-70
  name, 33
  obtaining, 32, 33
  packaging, 69
  pricing, 33-34
profit and cost projections, 40

radio, 63
records, keeping, 71-75
referrals, 85-86
regulatory bodies, 90-91
repeat business, 86
reputation, 97, 99
response, increasing, 77-82

sales letter, writing a, 46-54
servicing customers, 68-76
sole traders, 21-22
solicitors, 92-93
specialists, 91-93
stationery, 20
storage space, 15, 18

telephone technique, 20
television, 63
trading status, 21-22, 94
trading internationally, 100-101
traditional marketing, 12, 14
two step advertising, 43
typesetting, 62-63

unique selling proposition, 40-41

value, adding, 34, 70-71

working space, 18

HOW TO WRITE A PRESS RELEASE
A step-by-step guide to getting your message across

Peter Bartram

Every day, newspapers and magazines are deluged with thousands of press releases. Which stories make an editor sit and take up notice? Why do some press releases never get used? This book explains all. 'Takes you step-by-step through the process.' *Home Run Magazine*. 'Shows how to style and build a news story that carries value for readers...I recommend this book.' *Writers Forum*. 'Yes! Yes, yes, yes! Here at last is a book that tells it like it is.' *Writers Monthly*. 'Compulsory reading.' *Phoenix/AGCAS*. If you have ever had a press release rejected – or want to win 'free' column inches for your organisation – *How to Write a Press Release* is the handbook for you. Peter Bartram BSc(Econ) is one of Britain's most published business writers and journalists, with more than 2,500 feature articles and (seven books) to his credit. He edits the magazine *Executive Strategy*.

144pp illus. 1 85703 163 6. 2nd edition.

HOW TO BECOME A FREELANCE SALES AGENT
Your path to a more rewarding future

Terry James

The freelance sales agent is playing a bigger role in business today. As more and more companies shed employees to control costs, they are turning instead to independent sales agents, who can offer more flexible arrangements. This new book shows how anyone with good self-management skills and the determination to succeed can develop a great new career as a freelance sales agent. Using case histories, it illustrates how, by working for several firms, the sales agent can enjoy the real financial rewards and job satisfaction that comes from building their own client base. Terry James has himself been a successful sales agent for over ten years, specialising in products for the construction industry.

120pp illus. 1 85703 176 8.

HOW TO START YOUR OWN BUSINESS
Planning and creating a successful enterprise

Jim Green

This dynamic guide fully explores the vital steps to creating a business, interlaced with the author's recent experience in overcoming every hurdle encountered along the way in setting up his own business without capital or discretionary resources. It will show you how to galvanise into initial action, how to source proven ideas, how to write a winning plan, how to approach potential funders, how to present a case for public sector assistance, how to market your business and how to develop the selling habit. No matter what your age or personal circumstances, you *can* strike out on your own, create an enterprise and change your life for the better. Jim Green is chairman and managing director of Focus Publishing International Ltd and for many years specialised in founding, buying and selling advertising agencies.

159pp illus. 1 85703 122 9.

HOW TO PREPARE A BUSINESS PLAN
Laying the right foundations for business success

Matthew Record

A business plan is the most important commercial document you will ever have to produce, whether you are just starting out in business, or are already trading. A well thought out and carefully structured plan will be crucial to the survival and longterm success of the enterprise. It will provide a detailed map of exactly where it is going, and help you forestall any problems long before they arise. A third of all new businesses fail in their first year, and of the rest a staggering 95 per cent will not make it beyond 5 years. Poor planning has been identified as the major cause of business failure. With the odds so stacked against success, make sure YOUR business gets off to the right start. Matthew Record is a business consultant specialising in the preparation of business plans for a variety of commercial clients. His company, Phoenix Business Plans, is based in Dorset.

158pp illus. 1 85703 178 4.

How To Books

How To Books provide practical help on a large range of topics. They are available through all good bookshops or can be ordered direct from the distributors. Just tick the titles you want and complete the form on the following page.

___ Apply to an Industrial Tribunal (£7.99)
___ Applying for a Job (£7.99)
___ Applying for a United States Visa (£15.99)
___ Be a Freelance Journalist (£8.99)
___ Be a Freelance Secretary (£8.99)
___ Be a Local Councillor (£8.99)
___ Be an Effective School Governor (£9.99)
___ Become a Freelance Sales Agent (£9.99)
___ Become an Au Pair (£8.99)
___ Buy & Run a Shop (£8.99)
___ Buy & Run a Small Hotel (£8.99)
___ Cash from your Computer (£9.99)
___ Career Planning for Women (£8.99)
___ Choosing a Nursing Home (£8.99)
___ Claim State Benefits (£9.99)
___ Communicate at Work (£7.99)
___ Conduct Staff Appraisals (£7.99)
___ Conducting Effective Interviews (£8.99)
___ Copyright & Law for Writers (£8.99)
___ Counsel People at Work (£7.99)
___ Creating a Twist in the Tale (£8.99)
___ Creative Writing (£9.99)
___ Critical Thinking for Students (£8.99)
___ Do Voluntary Work Abroad (£8.99)
___ Do Your Own Advertising (£8.99)
___ Do Your Own PR (£8.99)
___ Doing Business Abroad (£9.99)
___ Emigrate (£9.99)
___ Employ & Manage Staff (£8.99)
___ Find Temporary Work Abroad (£8.99)
___ Finding a Job in Canada (£9.99)
___ Finding a Job in Computers (£8.99)
___ Finding a Job in New Zealand (£9.99)
___ Finding a Job with a Future (£8.99)
___ Finding Work Overseas (£9.99)
___ Freelance DJ-ing (£8.99)
___ Get a Job Abroad (£10.99)
___ Get a Job in America (£9.99)
___ Get a Job in Australia (£9.99)
___ Get a Job in Europe (£9.99)
___ Get a Job in France (£9.99)
___ Get a Job in Germany (£9.99)
___ Get a Job in Hotels and Catering (£8.99)
___ Get a Job in Travel & Tourism (£8.99)
___ Get into Films & TV (£8.99)
___ Get into Radio (£8.99)
___ Get That Job (£6.99)
___ Getting your First Job (£8.99)
___ Going to University (£8.99)
___ Helping your Child to Read (£8.99)
___ Investing in People (£8.99)
___ Invest in Stocks & Shares (£8.99)

___ Keep Business Accounts (£7.99)
___ Know Your Rights at Work (£8.99)
___ Know Your Rights: Teachers (£6.99)
___ Live & Work in America (£9.99)
___ Live & Work in Australia (£12.99)
___ Live & Work in Germany (£9.99)
___ Live & Work in Greece (£9.99)
___ Live & Work in Italy (£8.99)
___ Live & Work in New Zealand (£9.99)
___ Live & Work in Portugal (£9.99)
___ Live & Work in Spain (£7.99)
___ Live & Work in the Gulf (£9.99)
___ Living & Working in Britain (£8.99)
___ Living & Working in China (£9.99)
___ Living & Working in Hong Kong (£10.99)
___ Living & Working in Israel (£10.99)
___ Living & Working in Japan (£8.99)
___ Living & Working in Saudi Arabia (£12.99)
___ Living & Working in the Netherlands (£9.99)
___ Lose Weight & Keep Fit (£6.99)
___ Make a Wedding Speech (£7.99)
___ Making a Complaint (£8.99)
___ Manage a Sales Team (£8.99)
___ Manage an Office (£8.99)
___ Manage Computers at Work (£8.99)
___ Manage People at Work (£8.99)
___ Manage Your Career (£8.99)
___ Managing Budgets & Cash Flows (£9.99)
___ Managing Meetings (£8.99)
___ Managing Your Personal Finances (£8.99)
___ Market Yourself (£8.99)
___ Master Book-Keeping (£8.99)
___ Mastering Business English (£8.99)
___ Master GCSE Accounts (£8.99)
___ Master Languages (£8.99)
___ Master Public Speaking (£8.99)
___ Obtaining Visas & Work Permits (£9.99)
___ Organising Effective Training (£9.99)
___ Pass Exams Without Anxiety (£7.99)
___ Pass That Interview (£6.99)
___ Plan a Wedding (£7.99)
___ Prepare a Business Plan (£8.99)
___ Publish a Book (£9.99)
___ Publish a Newsletter (£9.99)
___ Raise Funds & Sponsorship (£7.99)
___ Rent & Buy Property in France (£9.99)
___ Rent & Buy Property in Italy (£9.99)
___ Retire Abroad (£8.99)
___ Return to Work (£7.99)
___ Run a Local Campaign (£6.99)
___ Run a Voluntary Group (£8.99)
___ Sell Your Business (£9.99)

___ Selling into Japan (£14.99)	___ Use the Internet (£9.99)
___ Setting up Home in Florida (£9.99)	___ Winning Consumer Competitions (£8.99)
___ Spend a Year Abroad (£8.99)	___ Winning Presentations (£8.99)
___ Start a Business from Home (£7.99)	___ Work from Home (£8.99)
___ Start a New Career (£6.99)	___ Work in an Office (£7.99)
___ Starting to Manage (£8.99)	___ Work in Retail (£8.99)
___ Starting to Write (£8.99)	___ Work with Dogs (£8.99)
___ Start Word Processing (£8.99)	___ Working Abroad (£14.99)
___ Start Your Own Business (£8.99)	___ Working as a Holiday Rep (£9.99)
___ Study Abroad (£8.99)	___ Working in Japan (£10.99)
___ Study & Learn (£7.99)	___ Working in Photography (£8.99)
___ Study & Live in Britain (£7.99)	___ Working in the Gulf (£10.99)
___ Studying at University (£8.99)	___ Working on Contract Worldwide (£9.99)
___ Studying for a Degree (£8.99)	___ Working on Cruise Ships (£9.99)
___ Successful Grandparenting (£8.99)	___ Write a CV that Works (£7.99)
___ Successful Mail Order Marketing (£9.99)	___ Write a Press Release (£9.99)
___ Successful Single Parenting (£8.99)	___ Write a Report (£8.99)
___ Survive at College (£4.99)	___ Write an Assignment (£8.99)
___ Survive Divorce (£8.99)	___ Write an Essay (£7.99)
___ Surviving Redundancy (£8.99)	___ Write & Sell Computer Software (£9.99)
___ Take Care of Your Heart (£5.99)	___ Write Business Letters (£8.99)
___ Taking in Students (£8.99)	___ Write for Publication (£8.99)
___ Taking on Staff (£8.99)	___ Write for Television (£8.99)
___ Taking Your A-Levels (£8.99)	___ Write Your Dissertation (£8.99)
___ Teach Abroad (£8.99)	___ Writing a Non Fiction Book (£8.99)
___ Teach Adults (£8.99)	___ Writing & Selling a Novel (£8.99)
___ Teaching Someone to Drive (£8.99)	___ Writing & Selling Short Stories (£8.99)
___ Travel Round the World (£8.99)	___ Writing Reviews (£8.99)
___ Use a Library (£6.99)	___ Your Own Business in Europe (£12.99)

To: Plymbridge Distributors Ltd, Plymbridge House, Estover Road, Plymouth PL6 7PZ.
Customer Services Tel: (01752) 202301. Fax: (01752) 202331.

Please send me copies of the titles I have indicated. Please add postage & packing
(UK £1, Europe including Eire, £2, World £3 airmail).

☐ I enclose cheque/PO payable to Plymbridge Distributors Ltd for £ _____

☐ Please charge to my ☐ MasterCard, ☐ Visa, ☐ AMEX card.

Account No. ☐☐☐☐☐☐☐☐☐☐☐☐☐☐☐

Card Expiry Date ☐☐ 19 ☎ **Credit Card orders may be faxed or phoned.**

Customer Name (CAPITALS) ....

Address ....

.... Postcode ....

Telephone .... Signature ....

Every effort will be made to despatch your copy as soon as possible but to avoid possible
disappointment please allow up to 21 days for despatch time (42 days if overseas). Prices
and availability are subject to change without notice.

Code BPA